Foreword

The Principles of Educational Psychology Series

The materials used to present educational psychology to teachers should have two dominant characteristics—excellence and adaptability. The *Principles of Educational Psychology Series* aspires to both. It consists of several short books, each devoted to an essential topic in the field. The authors of the books are responsible for their excellence; each author is noted for a command of his or her topic and for a deep conviction of the importance of the topic for teachers. Taken as a whole, the series provides comprehensive coverage of the major topics in educational psychology, but it is by no means a survey, for every topic is illuminated in a distinctive way by the individual approach of each author.

Numerous considerations require that the materials used

for instruction in educational psychology be adaptable. One consideration is that the readership is heterogeneous, including students in pre-service teacher training programs, of whom some have and others have not taken prior work in psychology, as well as professional teachers in in-service programs who have already completed previous courses in educational psychology. The separate booklets in the *Principles of Educational Psychology Series* are intended to be responsive to these differences. The writing is clear and direct, providing easy access for the novice, and the authors' fresh and distinctive viewpoints offer new insights to the more experienced.

Another consideration is that the format of courses in educational psychology varies widely. A course may be designed for pre-service or for in-service programs, for early childhood, elementary, secondary, or comprehensive programs, or to offer special preparation for teaching in urban, suburban, or rural settings. The course may occupy a full academic year, a semester, trimester, quarter, or an even shorter period. A common set of topics may be offered to all students in the course, or the topical coverage may be individualized. The *Principles of Educational Psychology Series* can be adapted to any one of these formats. Since the series consists of separate books, each one treating a single topic, instructors and students can choose to adopt the entire set or selected volumes from it, depending on the length, topical emphasis, and structure of the course.

The need for effective means of training teachers is of increasing urgency. To assist in meeting that need, the intent of the series is to provide materials for presenting educational psychology that are distinctive in approach, excellent in execution, and adaptable in use.

William Rohwer
Carol Rohwer
Series Editors
Berkeley, California
February, 1974

Preface

This is a book about human learning, intended to be useful to teachers and prospective teachers. I have tried to write plainly about a complex subject, including the most basic facts and principles, and illustrating these with examples of learning in educational settings. The resulting account seems to me to provide a framework that can serve well in organizing thought and the accumulation of knowledge about teaching. At the same time, I hope it will encourage students to continue to seek additional knowledge about human learning as it applies to the design and conduct of instruction.

Learning is described here in terms of the information-processing model of learning and memory, a model that underlies many contemporary theories. This model posits a number of internal processes that are subject to the influence of a variety of external events. The arrangement of external events to activate and support the internal processes of learning constitutes what is called instruction. The description of these external events and their effects on learning processes is the central theme of the book. Initial chapters deal with learning principles and are followed by chapters describing applications to the planning and delivery of instruction.

I have made a serious attempt to use language that is concrete and to provide illustrations of the principles being discussed. The account describes what learning psychologists have discovered only insofar as their findings illuminate the central theme. My intention is to tell the prospective teacher, "This is what will be most helpful for you to know about human learning."

Each chapter contains a concluding section, which has a distinctive topical heading. These sections summarize the chapter and also provide continuity with what is to come in the next. In addition, there are general references at the end of each chapter, arranged by topics, which can guide further study by the interested student. Specific references cited in the text are listed at the end of the book.

As a text, the book should find its greatest usefulness in undergraduate courses in educational psychology and as an adjunct to graduate offerings in this subject. It may also be appropriate as a supplementary text in courses in human learning, instructional methods, and applied psychology. In addition, the book may be a suitable component of courses and workshops offered as a part of the continuing education of teachers.

Robert M. Gagné
Tallahassee, Florida
February 1974

Contents

Essentials
of
Learning
for
Instruction

Chapter 1 Introduction

When students attend school or enroll in an educational program, they are assumed to be engaged in learning. Their activities may be highly varied, since they may be learning many different things—how to read a book, how to analyze a social problem, how to view a painting, how to play volleyball, and so on. Furthermore, a person may become a "student," and therefore be committed to learning, in any number of social contexts—a public school, a college, a study group, an adult class, a summer workshop, a series of night classes, a correspondence course. Despite the variety of these settings, there is evident in all of them a concern for learning.

The central purpose of any program of education is to *promote learning*. This is true whether one has in mind the learning of basic reading skills in children of age five or six, the acquiring of attitudes opposed to environmental pollution by teen-agers, or the attainment of knowledge of laws relating to real estate by adults of retirement age. The number of particular kinds of things that can be learned is vast, and the human life span during which learning can occur stretches from early childhood to extreme old age. A variety of educational institutions and programs are employed with the common aim of bringing about learning in human individuals.

Learning and the Teacher

Besides the student who is learning, the most important agent in an educational program is the teacher. It is the teacher's job to see that the various influences surrounding the student are selected and arranged to promote learning. Sometimes, as in the primary grades, this task must be planned in careful detail, taking into account the limitations of attention and comprehension of the students. In other situations, with older and more experienced students, the planning of conditions to promote learning can be done in larger "chunks" and can assume a greater share of responsibility on the part of the learner himself. The task of insuring that learning occurs changes with the age and experience of the learner but remains a constant part of the job of the teacher.

Teachers carry out the task of promoting learning by providing *instruction*. In fact, the word instruction may be defined as the set of events designed to initiate, activate, and support learning in a human learner. Such events must first be *planned*, and secondly they must be *delivered*, that is, made to have their effects on the learner. For example, the teacher may plan that a class of first grade students will learn some basic concepts like "in front of," "behind," "above," and "below." There is planning for the teacher's activity (introducing a pointing game, saying the words orally, varying the objects pointed to) and also for the student activity (playing the pointing game, repeating the word, verifying the direction of pointing, etc.). Instructional delivery follows: the children are assembled into a group, the various objects are identified, the group says each word in unison, individual players take their turns, and so on. In a ninth grade class the plan may be to have students learn by reading a chapter of a text on presidential conventions, with a review of major concepts following this self-study. The delivery may include an introductory statement by the teacher and a period containing questions directed to individual students (for example, "How does a person get to be a delegate?").

The responsibilities of planning and delivering instruction obviously require a knowledge of the *process of learning*. If the aim of instruction is to promote learning, the teacher must have some idea of what learning is and how it occurs. In order to plan events external to the learner which will activate and support learning, one must gain a conception of what is going on "inside the learner's head." That is what knowledge of the principles of learning and learning theory provides. Sections of this chapter will introduce some of these conceptions, and later chapters will expand upon them.

What a Teacher Needs to Know About Learning

Teachers are bombarded by communications from many quarters claiming to help promote learning. Advertisements for textbooks, school equipment, teachers' manuals and handbooks, and many other sources offer varied suggestions about how learning can best be achieved. Since teachers are often faced with the problem of choosing among educational products, it is necessary for them to judge these claims, preferably in terms of their likely validity. A sound knowledge of verified learning principles and learning theory will aid in the choice process. Of course, such knowledge can be employed to even greater effect in evaluating educational products that are directly examined or tried out with students.

Teachers customarily plan "lessons" or "learning units" to be undertaken by their students, often using purchased materials (texts, workbooks, etc.) as a framework for their planning. In addition, teachers or teams of teachers sometimes plan entire courses with outlines or syllabi of lesson topics. In the elementary grades, teachers often plan lessons that include materials they themselves develop and fabricate. Knowledge of learning principles and theory is of great importance in these activities. When performing these tasks, the teacher is the *designer* of instruction and should be highly knowledgeable about those learning principles which will insure the success of what is planned.

The teacher is the *manager* of instruction, seeing to it that instruction is effectively delivered to the student, whether by oral communication, reading, or some other medium. This means that the teacher must arrange the conditions for learning in such a way that each and every student will learn what is intended. The proper structuring of the learning environment to insure that students achieve the educational objectives is a demanding activity which is critically dependent upon knowledge of learning processes.

The third primary function of the teacher in promoting learning is as an *evaluator* of student learning. On a day-to-day and even a minute-to-minute basis, the effective teacher maintains a concern about what each student has learned and decides how to arrive at valid conclusions regarding the outcomes of learning. In playing this role, the teacher designs situations that require the student to demonstrate what he has learned. Often this is done by asking questions, by describing problems for the student to solve, or by setting incomplete tasks for the student to finish. On other occasions, usually over longer intervals, student learning may be evaluated by quizzes or tests. Obviously, successful evaluation of learning is greatly dependent upon a knowledge of what kinds of outcomes may be expected from the process of learning.

The Nature of Learning

Learning is something that takes place inside an individual's head—in his brain. Learning is called a *process* because it is formally comparable to other human organic processes such as digestion and respiration. However, learning is an enormously intricate and complex process, which is only partially understood at present. As is true for other organic processes, knowledge about learning can be accumulated by scientific methods. When adequately verified, such knowledge can be expressed as *learning principles*. And when these principles, in turn, can be seen to hang together in a way that makes rational sense, a *model* of the learning process can be constructed. The elaborations of this model (or of alternative models) are what is known as *learning theories*.

In subsequent sections of this chapter, we shall have more to say about learning principles and models and how they are derived. First, however, we must state our definition of learning.

A Definition of Learning

What is learning, and how do we know when it is occurring? Evidently, learning is a process of which certain kinds of living organisms are capable—many animals, including human beings, but not plants. It is a process which enables these organisms to modify their behavior fairly rapidly in a more or less permanent way, so that the same modification does not have to occur again and again in each new situation. An external observer can recognize that learning has happened when he notes the occurrence of *behavioral change* and also the *persistence* of this change. Inferred from such observations is a new "persisting state" achieved by the learner.

There is, however, one major class of persistent behavioral change which is not learning and that is *maturation*— changes resulting from the growth of internal structures. The behavioral change which can be observed in the infant's use of his eyes, for example, or the child's progressive development of muscular coordination are attributable to maturation. The sexual functioning of the human being is likewise a matter of maturation, dependent upon growth of underlying structures at the time of puberty. It is essential to distinguish these kinds of behavioral change from those called learning. Whereas learning typically occurs when the individual responds to and receives stimulation from his external environment, maturation requires only internal growth. The persisting behavioral change called learning, then, must be confined to that which occurs when the organism *interacts* with his external environment. As we shall see later, the capacity for learning reaches such a high level in human beings that certain types of interaction can be represented internally and therefore can take place entirely "in the head."

The important characteristics of learning can readily be gleaned from the description introduced up to this point. Learning is a *process* of which man and other animals are capable. It typically involves *interaction* with the external environment (or a representation of this interaction, as noted previously). Learning is inferred when a change or *modification in behavior* occurs, which *persists* over relatively long periods during the life of the individual. These definitional statements show us that gaining an understanding of learning, which is the primary aim for readers of this book, requires seeking answers to the following questions:

1. What is the nature of the internal process (or processes) involved in learning?

2. What kinds of human behavior can be modified by learning?

3. What are the characteristics of the persisting "states" that result from learning?

4. How can one identify and describe the learner-environment interaction that distinguishes learning? In other words, what are the conditions for learning?

5. How does one know when learning has occurred?

These are the major questions this book attempts to answer. In addition, because our orientation is a highly practical one, we shall be giving an important share of attention to the following question pertaining to the teacher's role in the promotion of learning:

6. How can a knowledge of learning be applied to the planning and delivery of instruction?

All these questions focus primary attention on the individual human learner, and on the fundamental principle that learning takes place within the individual. The environment of the learner often includes a teacher as well as other learners. The teacher has many things to do and may be engaging in activities that promote learning in a number of different learners at once. The other learners in the situation, whether they are interacting as a group, in teams or pairs, or as individuals, may be learning the same things, different things, or may not even be learning. To understand and recognize the learning that is taking place, one must relate these various features of the environment to the process that is expected to occur in the individual learner.

Knowledge about Learning

Where does knowledge about learning come from? To be useful, knowledge about learning must be both *reliable* and *valid*. Facts about learning are reliable when the same fact can be observed again and again under the same conditions; in other words, when it is dependable. To be valid, an item of knowledge must be applicable to a range of situations. It must not be so "special" that it has no breadth of application to situations other than the one where it was first observed. Knowledge with these characteristics is obtained by scientific methods. It is obtained by observation; but the observation must be repeated, conducted under conditions which control the limits of its generality, and verified.

It might seem that a most economical way to obtain knowledge about learning would be to ask the learner or perhaps a set of learners. A limited amount of information can in fact be obtained in this way. But, in general, a learner is simply not aware of the internal processes that occur when he is learning and so cannot report them. He may be aware of some results of these processes or of some decisions he makes about these results. However, even when learners have been asked to report these events, it is often found that they are not reliable; that is, they vary in consistency from time to time and from learner to learner. For these reasons, the learner's own reports are not generally considered to be good sources of knowledge about learning.

When sound knowledge of the events of learning is sought, observations are usually made on an individual or a group of learners who are given a particular task to do, and whose behavior can then be observed under specified conditions. Generally, the people who carry out studies of learning in this manner are psychologists. As is well known, psychologists devote themselves to the study of mental processes, and the processes of learning constitute an important portion of the operations of the mind, as these are reflected in behavior. The learning psychologist plans and conducts studies of learning in order to determine and describe its properties; in other words, in order to gain knowledge about learning which is both reliable and valid.

A learning psychologist may be interested in discovering knowledge which will answer any or all of the questions listed in the previous section. He may be interested, for example, in what mental processes are involved when a child learns to identify printed letters or read words; in the extent to which such behaviors can be modified by learning; in the nature of the persisting state the child acquires through learning; and in what conditions are necessary to bring about such learning. He sets about finding this knowledge by observing a set of children (usually one at a time) who are in a situation controlled in specified ways, who are presented with a specified set of materials (printed letters, words), and in whom modifications of behavior can be observed. He records these observations and searches out the consistent trends among them—in other words, the aspects of behavior which recur again and again and are therefore reliable. Since he is unable to make direct ob-

servations on the *process* of learning, he must make inferences about this process. These inferences are abstractions
from the raw observations he makes—they constitute generalized knowledge and are often called *learning principles*.
The psychologist must then verify his learning principles.
This is done by deducing one or more additional learning
outcomes as observations to be made in a newly specified
situation, sometimes with still another set of learners.
When predicted outcomes correspond with observed outcomes, the principles are said to be verified, and such
observations support the conclusion that the principles are
valid.

An Example of the Study of Learning

Let us illustrate the procedures of gaining knowledge
about learning with a particular example. The learning
psychologist in this case was interested in children learning
some facts of natural science, of the sort that commonly
appear in science courses in the elementary grades (Gagné,
1969). To represent this kind of learning task, he constructed some paragraphs of printed text pertaining to
howling monkeys and their habits of life. Each paragraph
was made up of five short sentences, and each concerned a
particular topic about howling monkeys. There were five
paragraphs in all, and their topics were (1) play,
(2) mother-child relationships, (3) actions toward enemies,
(4) the howler's tail, and (5) forest living.

Each sentence of the paragraphs was projected on a
screen at the front of the room and read to the children.
Two days later, each child wrote answers to questions
based on the text by supplying missing words in type-
written sentences (which were also read aloud by the
teacher).

For one group of children, the paragraphs were made to
contain *topic sentences*; for another equivalent group, they
did not contain topic sentences. For example, in one group
the paragraph on howler play began with the sentence,
"Howlers have many forms of play." For the other group

of children, the paragraph was not begun with a topic sentence, but only with another sentence pertaining to the topic (such as "Howler children swing by their tails from tree branches").

The learning investigator in this instance was attempting to test a hypothesis (that is, a proposed learning principle) having to do with the *conditions* of learning, which he hoped would also provide evidence about the *process* of learning. Specifically, he was interested in observing whether individual facts occurring in paragraphs would be more readily learned if the paragraphs contained an initial organizing sentence than if the paragraphs had no such topic sentence. For example, would a fact like "Young howlers wrestle and chase each other in play" be more readily learned if the paragraph in which it occurred had an initial topic sentence which announced that the paragraph was concerned with howler play activities; Or would it be learned better if it occurred within a paragraph beginning with another specific fact about howler play, not a topic sentence?

Many factors in the learning situation for this study had to be controlled in order for suitable observations to be made. Among other things, the background and learning aptitude of the children who learned with topic sentences had to be made equivalent to that of the children who learned without topic sentences. Differences in reading ability among the children was eliminated as an influencing factor by having the sentences read to the children. The time for viewing and hearing each of the sentences in the paragraph was concerned with howler play activities? Or was allowed for each child to print or write his answer to each of the test questions given two days following the learning session, and it was known that the children were able to perform such a task. The children fell within a narrow range of ages in grades 4 and 5.

The results of this learning study, illustrated graphically in Figure 1.1, show that the children who learned from paragraphs containing topic sentences recalled a higher percentage of individual facts than did those who were not given topic sentences.

Figure 1.1
Average scores in the recall of facts by groups of fourth and fifth grade children, from paragraphs with and without topic sentences.

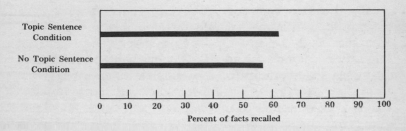

From Gagné, 1969.

Reliability. The controlled observation of this study shows, then, that a paragraph with a topic sentence, when presented to fourth and fifth grade children, yields better retention of facts within it than does a paragraph without a topic sentence. Is this a *reliable* observation? This question was answered in this study, as is often customary, by providing for *repeated observations*. The investigator observed not the learning of a fact from a single paragraph, but the learning of five different facts from five different paragraphs, each concerned with a different topic (about howling monkeys), and each having a different topic sentence appropriate to it. Since the investigator was interested in drawing a general conclusion about the effects of a topic sentence, he attempted to insure that his observations would be made repeatedly, on several instances of topic sentences.

Validity. Is the conclusion about the effect of a topic sentence a *valid* one? This is a slightly more complex question to answer. One answer comes from the observation that the retention scores of children given a topic sentence were higher than those of (equivalent) children who were not given a topic sentence. How much higher were these scores, only a little or a great deal? In actuality, they were found to be "significantly" higher, as established by a statistical measure which permits the investigator to reject the idea that such differences could have occurred by *chance*.

However, the question of validity concerns more than statistical significance. Would the principle about a topic sentence apply to any kind of paragraphs, any length of text, or any kind of student? Obviously we must be more cautious about validity of the principle when we are making generalizations. Additional studies with other observations will be needed to increase our confidence about the limits of applicability of the principle. The principle is valid, but this is not an all-or-none matter; it is valid under conditions that are not unreasonably different from those under which it was verified.

Controlling conditions.   The necessity for making controlled observations means that the investigator of the learning process must make suitable arrangements for the selection of learners for his study and of the environment in which they learn. Sometimes the need for controls is such that he must deal with individual learners in an isolated room, perhaps a "laboratory" room or a single learning carrel. On other occasions, as in the example just described, it is possible to conduct the study in one or more classrooms or in other assembly rooms within a school. The materials used to present the learning task must also often be specially constructed in order to be appropriately controlled; in other instances, lessons presented in the normal course of instruction may be suitable. Often the most difficult factor to control in learning studies is the aptitude and learning background of the learners. When conducted in schools, studies usually require that a special effort be made to control the equivalence of students in these characteristics.

A principle of learning. Besides the knowledge the topic-sentence study yielded about the conditions of learning, was anything revealed about learning as a process? Again the answer is affirmative but must be carefully qualified. Making inferences about the process of learning can seldom be confidently done from the results of a single study. What is suggested by this example is that facts are learned more readily when they can be meaningfully related by the learner to broader generalizations. Thus, the single fact "Mother howler monkeys carry their babies with them wherever they go" is better learned and remembered if it can be related to the generalization "Howler mothers take good care of their babies." The suggestion is therefore implied that the learning (storage) of facts involves a *process of organizing* these facts. To be learned most effectively, individual facts must be "subsumed" in a larger meaningful context (Ausubel, 1968). But, obviously, the existence of such a "subsumption process," as well as its properties, must be inferred from a great many studies. Accordingly, those who study the process of learning usually conduct not single studies but whole series of studies. Each study in a series may contribute some small amount of knowledge about the process of learning, while at the same time confirming other pieces of knowledge. (Several additional examples of investigations of human learning are described in the volume of this series by Reese.)

Learning Theory

The results of learning studies yield an accumulation of learning *principles* which can be repeatedly verified. These principles contribute to a body of knowledge about learning which continues to grow in breadth and precision. Principles discovered in this manner often suggest ways of organizing a number of disparate facts into a single conceptualization called a *theory*. A learning theory is designed to provide an explanation of several (sometimes many) specific facts which have been independently observed, by relating these facts to a conceptual *model*. The model itself cannot be directly observed, but it may generate a number of consequences that can be. To the extent that these consequences are progressively verified, usually over a period of years, the learning theory becomes increasingly "well established" and more frequently employed as an explanation.

A Historical Example

In 1921, a leading investigator of learning, E. L. Thorndike, proposed as a major component of his learning theory the Law of Exercise (Thorndike, 1921, p. 2). This principle stated that a learned connection was "strengthened" each time it was repeated. (It should be noted that the strengthening of a connection was also dependent upon other principles, according to Thorndike. Among these was the Law of Effect, nowadays referred to as "reinforcement.") A number of learned performances were used to illustrate and test Thorndike's principle—adding numbers, mental multiplication, memorizing numbers and names, handwriting, and others. Generally, the evidence showed that repeated practice of a task such as adding columns of figures improved the performance of learners; they completed more problems correctly in stated intervals of time (say, five minutes). The basic theoretical idea, in other words, was that repeated practice improved performance because a set of "connections" was "strengthened."

Thorndike's Law of Exercise has persisted for many years and still may be shown to have validity under some conditions. The more general theory of which this principle is a part has also shown great persistence. Over the years, however, evidence has accumulated to indicate that learning is *not* fundamentally a matter of gradual strengthening of connections but rather an all-or-none event. Thus most modern theorists tend to favor the idea that the individual connection is acquired on a single occasion (Estes,

1964). The effects of repetition may be to recruit more and more single connections, but each one is either learned or not learned. Of course, this more modern theory does not deny that improvement often (though not always) results from practice. It does deny that improvement depends on a *strengthening process*. Thus, from accumulating evidence and periodic questioning of assumptions, learning theory assumes new forms over the years.

Modern Learning Theory and Its Model

The theory of learning most prominently displayed in this book is of a variety known as "information-processing theory." According to this type of theory, the processes that one must conceive in order to explain the phenomena of learning are those that make certain kinds of *transformations* of "inputs" to "outputs" in a fashion somewhat analogous to the workings of a computer. For instance, when a learner is in a learning situation, physical stimulation of his eyes, ears, and other senses is transformed into certain neural "messages." The messages in turn undergo other transformations in the nervous system, so that they can be stored and later recalled. The recalled information is again transformed into still other kinds of "messages" which control the action of the muscles. The result is speech or other types of movement indicating that a performance has been learned. These various forms of transformation are called *learning processes*; they are what goes on "inside the learner's head." It is these processes, their characteristics and their manner of functioning, which constitute the essence of modern learning theory.

A basic model of learning and memory, representing the essential features of most modern learning theories, is shown in Figure 1.2. To the right of "receptors" and "effectors," the model shows the structures postulated to exist in the central nervous system of the learner. These structures are presumed to be neural networks, but their locations have not yet been precisely determined (see Lindsay & Norman, 1972).

The model shown in Figure 1.2 is the basis for our dis-

Figure 1.2
The basic model of learning and memory
underlying modern "information-processing"
theories.

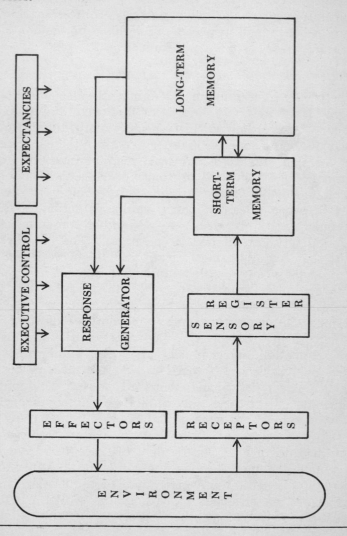

cussion of learning processes and their implications for instruction in the later chapters of this book. At this point, we do not expect the reader to acquire a full understanding of the model, just an acquaintance with its major features. Perhaps it will be possible for the reader to acquire a "mental picture" of Figure 1.2, so that he can follow the *flow* of information and capture the idea that it is *processed* (transformed) in various ways as it passes from one structure to another.

The flow of information. Stimulation from the learner's *environment* affects his *receptors* and enters the nervous system via a *sensory register*. This is the structure responsible for the initial perception of objects and events that the learner sees, hears, or otherwise senses. The information is "coded" in the sensory register, that is, it has the form of a patterned representation of the original stimulation. The information remains in this form for only the smallest fraction of a second.

Entering the *short-term* memory, the information is again coded, this time into a conceptual form. Thus, a figure like X becomes a representation such as an "X"; a figure like ·· becomes the concept "two" (not the word *two*). Persistence in the short-term memory is relatively brief, a matter of seconds. However, the information may be processed by *internal rehearsal* and thus preserved in the short-term memory for longer periods. Rehearsal may also play a part in another operation: if the information is to be remembered, it is once again transformed and enters the long-term memory, where it is stored for later recall. Most theories assume that storage in long-term memory is permanent and that later failures to recall result from difficulties of "finding" the information.

It is important to note that the short-term and long-term memories may not actually be different structures, but only different ways of functioning of the same structure. Notice also that information that has passed from the short-term memory to the long-term memory may be *re-*

trieved back to short-term memory. The latter is sometimes spoken of as the "working memory" or the "con-
scious memory." When new learning depends partly on the
recall of something that has previously been learned, this
something must be retrieved from long-term memory and
must reenter the short-term memory.

Information from either short-term or long-term memory, when retrieved, passes to a *response generator*, which
has the function of transforming the information into action. The neural "message" from this structure activates
the effectors (muscles), producing a performance which
affects the learner's environment. This action is what enables the external observer to tell that the stimulation has
had its expected effect—that the "information has been
processed," and the learner has indeed learned.

The processing of information.   A very important set of
structures shown in Figure 1.2 has yet to be described.
These are labeled *executive control* and *expectancies*. Sig-
nals from these structures are presumed to activate and
modify the flow of information. For example, the learner
has an expectancy of what he will be able to do once he
has learned, and this in turn may affect how an external
stimulus is perceived, how it is coded in memory, and how
it is transformed into action. *Control processes* originating
in the executive control structure may determine how the
information is coded when it enters long-term memory and
how the search and retrieval are conducted for recall,
among other things. (References to various theoretical
accounts are: Atkinson & Shiffrin, 1968; Norman, 1970;
Anderson & Bower, 1972; Lindsay & Norman, 1972).

The ways in which learning occurs are critically influenced by processes initiated in the executive control and
expectancy structures. The *flow* of information is one
aspect of the learning model—the *control* of this flow,
which determines the transformations ("codings") the
information undergoes, is quite another. In later chapters,
we shall have more to say about expectancies and also

about control processes, which we refer to as *cognitive strategies*.

A note about learning theory.   A learning theory attempts to postulate as few different processes as possible and to endow each with as few properties as possible, while still managing to explain the phenomena of learning. In this sense, it is generally thought that the simplest theory is the best. However, the simplest model may not always be adequate to explain the phenomena to which it is addressed, and when this happens the learning theorist faces the necessity of adding additional features or choosing a more complex model. There is always a justifiable reluctance to do this since the loss of simplicity brings with it a loss of clarity and explanatory power. Thorndike's Law of Exercise, for example, was investigated countless times in studies of learning extending over many years. When the evidence revealed more and more instances in which repetition failed to "strengthen the connection," as shown by improved learning or retention, the effects of repetition on learning had to be explained by a newer and more complex theory. The newer theory is in greater accord with observations of learning and is therefore more widely accepted despite its relative loss of simplicity.

The Usefulness of Learning Theory

Of what use is learning theory to the teacher? How can it help in the day-to-day performance of the many tasks the teacher is expected to do? These important questions deserve to be considered and answered by those who choose teaching as a profession. Since the promotion of learning is still the central purpose of educational programs, it is a central responsibility of the teachers involved in these programs. How can learning theory help teachers promote learning?

First of all, it is possible to have false expectations concerning the application of learning principles and learning theory to the job of teaching. One irrational expectation is that knowledge of learning can be applied to virtually all the teacher's activities in designing lessons or conducting classes. It is easy to show that this cannot be the case. A designer of bridges, for example, must be highly aware of the physical theory limiting the force that can be applied to certain masses; yet, in the details of design, he depends on practical knowledge of structures and materials as well as some ideals of esthetic quality. Similarly, the builder of a bridge uses many procedures that must be soundly based in physical principles, yet he does not derive them anew each time he puts them into practice. In an analogous fashion, the teacher who designs a lesson or conducts a class is practicing arts that are derived from many sources of practical knowledge as well as principles and theories of the learning process.

Another kind of false expectation about the application of learning theory is the notion that the right theory or principle will provide a "magic key" to teaching. The variety of situations that characterize instruction make it impossible for a theory with general applicability to determine the details of instructional procedures in a constant manner. Sometimes, for example, repetition is a procedure which promotes learning; sometimes it does not. Sometimes it is valuable to ask students to learn new concepts by "discovering" them; sometimes it is better to "tell" what the concepts are. In certain cases, learning is better promoted by asking questions of students; on other occasions it may be better to have students formulate questions. An understanding of learning theory does not lead to the use of standardized procedures of instruction, nor is it likely to furnish a "single best" procedure that can be applied in all teaching situations.

On the other hand, the following points outline what a knowledge of learning theory *can* reasonably be expected to do for a teacher:

1. In the *planning* of lessons and courses, learning principles disclose the limits of what is possible in instruction. For example, if what is to be learned is the ability to

spell new words, such learning is not possible, according to theory, by repeated practice on words whose spelling is already familiar to the learner. Regardless of what other conditions may be present, including high motivation of teacher and student, the latter procedure is not within the limits suggested by learning principles and can therefore be ruled out immediately. According to learning theory, the teacher must adequately identify what behavior is involved in spelling new words before deciding on the conditions of instruction.

2. In the *conduct* of instruction, a knowledge of learning theory can guide the teacher's choice of action. For example, if a student mumbles while making an oral report to the class, it is most useful to consider what he must learn in order to overcome this tendency. In contrast, it is of little use to conclude that he is being foolish or stubborn. Analyzing the situation to discover what learning is needed suggests to the teacher what the next step in instruction ought to be. Again, learning theory provides the knowledge of what alternatives are possible and how they may be undertaken to promote the necessary learning.

3. In *assessing* what has been learned, principles of learning make possible the means of comparing what students are able to do with what they are expected to have learned (that is, with "objectives"). For example, if students are expected to learn the meaning of the "due process" clause in the U.S. Constitution, a knowledge of learning principles enables the teacher to use procedures which will reveal whether the desired meaning has or has not been learned. Obviously, asking the question "Do you know what 'due process' means?" will not accomplish the purpose. The kinds of questions, and the kinds of student performances, that *are* capable of assessing such learning can be derived from verified learning principles.

These uses of knowledge of theories and principles of learning demonstrate that such knowledge guides the various activities of the teacher in planning and managing instruction. While learning theory cannot be expected to determine step-by-step procedures, it nevertheless provides direction, options, and priorities for the teacher's actions. When teachers verify their activities against the standards of learning theory, they are accomplishing two highly desirable things. First, they are avoiding the grossly inappropriate actions which, although seemingly desirable on other grounds, nevertheless fail to promote learning in students. And second, they are adopting and maintaining attitudes which support learning as the central purpose of their activities. In the face of many potential distractions in the practice of teaching, the teacher keeps student learning as a primary focus of concern.

Topics of the Book

As people concerned with the selection of instructional materials and the design, management, and evaluation of instruction, teachers are aided by their knowledge of learning principles and theories. It is the purpose of this book to convey this knowledge in the most fundamental sense. Of course, we cannot describe all there is to know about learning since that would require many books. However, as we indicated earlier in this chapter, the essentials that the teacher needs to know are treated as follows in this volume:

1. What is meant by learning, how knowledge of learning is obtained, and the basic model underlying modern learning theories have been described in this introductory chapter. In addition, we have tried to show why such knowledge is of value to the teacher in the various roles he performs and to suggest how such knowledge can be used to guide the planning and conduct of instruction.

2. The next topic to be considered, in Chapter 2, is the *processes* involved in learning. What is it that takes place inside the learner when an act of learning occurs? What kinds of events take place in the learner's environment that provide support for learning? Given the existence of these processes with their accompanying events, what can be

said about the arrangement of conditions for the promotion of learning?

3. What kinds of "persisting states" are learned? This question requires a consideration of the kinds of human performance which may be modified by learning. These are the learnable *capabilities* of human beings, described in Chapter 3. In addition, the implications of these principles for identifying classes of learning "objectives" are described.

4. Having distinguished the outcomes of learning, we proceed in Chapter 4 to deal with questions such as: What *conditions* are necessary to bring about learning aimed at each of these types of outcome? What can be done to make learning effective and also efficient? Other questions dealt with in this chapter pertain to the conditions affecting retention of learning and the transfer of learning to other tasks and situations.

5. How can knowledge of learning principles be used in *planning instruction*? This is the subject of Chapter 5, which considers planning in terms of the course, the lesson, and the events within a lesson. Planning is based on the objectives of instruction and the arrangement of instructional events to activate and support learning processes.

6. How can learning principles be applied to the *delivery of instruction*? In Chapter 6, consideration is given to group and individual activities in learning and the control of instruction by the learner. As an essential part of instructional management, the selection and use of audiovisual media is also dealt with in this chapter.

The purpose of the book as a whole should by now be clear. It is to describe essential principles of learning. This is done in order to provide teachers (or those who intend to become teachers) with knowledge useful in the selection and design of instructional procedures and materials, the management of instruction, and the assessment of its outcomes. All these areas of teacher decision-making relate to the promotion of learning.

A note about references. At the end of each chapter are listed a number of general references related to the topics discussed. These are books or general articles that will enable the reader to investigate more thoroughly matters of special interest to him. In addition, specific references cited in the text are listed at the end of the book.

General References

Learning Fundamentals

Deese, J., & Hulse, S. H. *The psychology of learning.* (3rd ed.) New York: McGraw-Hill, 1967.

Gagné, R. M. *The conditions of learning.* (2nd ed.) New York: Holt, Rinehart & Winston, 1970.

Hilgard, E. R., & Bower, G. H. *Theories of learning* (4th ed.) New York: Appleton-Century-Crofts, 1974.

Travers, R. M. W. *Essentials of learning* (3rd ed.) New York: Macmillan, 1972.

Models of Learning and Memory

Lindsay, P. H., & Norman, D. A. *Human information processing: An introduction to psychology.* New York: Academic Press, 1972.

Norman, D. A. (Ed.) *Models of human memory.* New York: Academic Press, 1970.

Tulving, E., & Donaldson, W. (Eds.) *Organization of memory.* New York: Academic Press, 1972.

The Roles of the Teacher

Glaser, R. Learning and the technology of instruction. *AV Communication Review,* 1961, 9, 42-55.

Nuthall, G., & Snook, I. Contemporary models of teaching. In R. M. W. Travers (Ed.), *Second handbook of research on teaching.* Chicago: Rand McNally, 1973.

Smith, B. O. A concept of teaching. *Teachers College Record,* 1960, 61, 229-241.

Chapter 2 The Processes of Learning

As indicated by the model introduced in Chapter 1, learning occurs as a result of the interaction between a learner and his environment. We know learning has taken place when we observe that the learner's performance has been modified. At one moment in time, for example, a child may not be able to point to the correct article of furniture when we ask him the question, "Where is the credenza?" When we then indicate the credenza to him together with its name, we provide the opportunity for the interaction called learning to take place. Later, we ask the question again, and the child now identifies the object. By means of this set of observations, we see the *change* in the child's behavior, and we make the immediate inference that *learning* has taken place.

The set of events observed as learning is formally similar

whether we are dealing with changes in the performances of riding a bicycle, recounting the provisions of the Dred Scott decision, cooking peanut brittle, composing a grammatically correct sentence, solving a differential equation, or interpreting a building code. Countless performances are modified during the course of an individual lifetime, and most of these changes result from learning. The performances themselves vary greatly in kind and in the situations in which they occur; yet it is possible to identify and describe some common features of the events of learning. It is these common characteristics of learning with which the present chapter is concerned.

Some of the events that make up a learning incident are *external* to the learner. These are the readily observable things: the stimulation that reaches the learner and the products (including written and spoken information) that result from his responding. In addition, many learning events are *internal* to the learner and are inferred from the observations made externally. These internal activities, which are considered to take place in the learner's central nervous system, are called *processes* of learning. These processes are implied by the transition points between each set of structures of the basic learning model shown in Figure 1.2.

The Events of Learning

Let us look more closely at the events, both external and internal, that transpire when learning takes place. There is, of course, a moment in time when the learner's internal state changes from not-learned to learned, which we will call the *essential incident* of learning. However, this incident is preceded by certain events that lead up to it and are no less fundamental to the total learning act. The essential incident is also followed by other events, also parts of the total act, which have to do with the execution of the performance that learning has made possible. Considering a single act of learning as a whole, then, it is necessary to describe a set of events that occupy at least a number of seconds and sometimes several minutes.

The typical series of events that constitute a single act of learning is shown in Figure 2.1. This figure outlines eight phases into which a single act of learning may be analyzed. Each phase has been given a name, and under each phase name appears a box identifying the principal *process* considered operative during that phase. What we have done, in short, amounts to two things. First, we have spread out the internal processes of learning, as implied by the structures of Figure 1.2, into a single chain. These processes are shown in the boxes of Figure 2.1. Second, we have considered each of these processes as a *phase* of an act of learning and given them appropriate labels. These labels (motivation phase, etc.) serve to relate the internal processes to the external events that constitute instruction; that is, they provide names for the total set of events (internal and external) that must be considered to take place during each phase of learning.

The phases of learning shown in Figure 2.1 cannot necessarily be easily observed under everyday circumstances. Special experimental controls and specially designed learning situations are necessary in order to study any one or any combination of the phases in terms of its separate effects on the learning act. Such study, of course, is often the purpose of scientific investigations of learning.

Another caution needs to be made in interpreting the information shown in Figure 2.1. This is the fact that the learner is not aware, and apparently cannot be aware, of most of the processes of learning. Introspective accounts of what is happening internally during an act of learning have not been successful in revealing these processes. Usually, the learner's reports of his own processes are quite uninformative. It needs to be borne in mind that the processes and phases outlined in Figure 2.1 result from many years of controlled observations of people who are engaged in learning, followed by rational construction of "what must be going on." These conclusions could not have been reached by a learning investigator examining his own mind.

Figure 2.1
The phases of an act of learning, and
the processes associated with them.

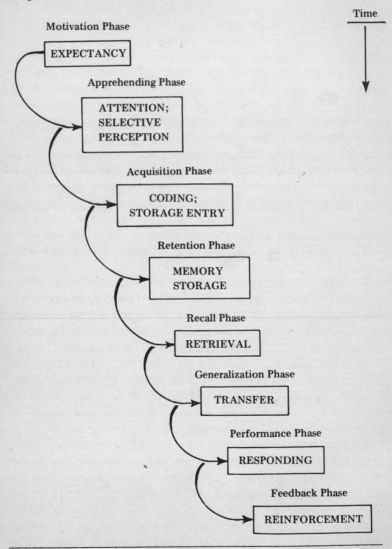

Even though the processes of learning are not directly observable, they nevertheless can be subjected to influences from the learner's environment. This is what a "learning situation" amounts to in practice: the teacher brings to bear certain external factors which influence the processes of learning. Thus, events may be made to occur which affect the motivation of the learner, his attention, or any of the other processes which make up the total learning act. When used to promote learning, these external influences together constitute the procedures of instruction.

Motivation Phase

It is a truism that in order for learning to occur, one must have a motivated individual. But there are many forms of motivation, some of which are relevant to learning and instruction, and others which are not. For the promotion of learning, we must deal primarily with *incentive motivation*, a type of motivation in which the individual strives to *achieve* some goal and is in some sense rewarded for reaching it. His action is proceeding toward an achievable goal. Incentive motivation is involved in many school and classroom situations. The student who has begun a project on Greek sculpture wants to achieve the goal of completing it. The student who has begun to solve simultaneous algebraic equations wants to be able to do all such problems correctly, that is, to attain an answer which will "check out." The youngster in the first grade wants to learn about the strange new shell his classmate is showing and describing, because he can then ask a "good" question about it or perhaps later tell his parents about it.

Incentive motivation has been called a variety of names, including "achievement motivation," "effectance," and the "urge for mastery." Some psychologists view it as a fundamental human urge, and one which is broadly involved in the behavior of human beings (White, 1959). Presumably, it reflects the natural tendency of the human being to manipulate, dominate, and "master" his environment. This is what an individual does when he makes something, rearranges things, completes something he has fabricated, or creates something that did not previously exist. For the learning that takes place in the educational environment, the goals that are possible to achieve are many and varied—completing a problem, printing a message, writing an essay, constructing a model of a city, making a high score in a basketball game. All these activities may lead to achievable goals that engender learning.

Establishing motivation. On other occasions, the learner may not be initially motivated by the incentive of achieving a goal. In these cases, the second alternative to action comes into play: one must *establish* the motivation, rather than simply verify that it is present. As is implied by Figure 2.1, motivation may be established by generating within the learner a process called *expectancy*, which is an anticipation of the "reward" he will obtain when he achieves some goal (Estes, 1972). In a human learner, an expectancy can be established by communicating to him the nature of the incentive or goal; that is, the expectancy is what he expects to happen as a consequence of his learning activity. For example, the learner may be told that when his learning is completed, he will be able to distinguish good art from bad, to appraise the value of a piece of real estate, or to repair a television set.

Alternatively, it may be necessary for the individual to acquire the desired expectancy by learning, rather than by simply being told. The younger the learner, the more likely it is that communicating the incentive will not be sufficiently effective to establish motivation. The expectancy may need to be learned in a more direct way. The learner acquires an expectancy when his attainment of a goal is rewarded. In order to generate such expectancies, situations can be arranged that permit learners to reach intended goals before they have actually acquired necessary skills. Thus, one can guide a student through the steps of a mathematics problem and then show him that he has "found the answer." This situation provides a reward, and consequently tends to generate an expectancy which will motivate the student to learn how to solve such problems. As another example, one can help a child to form the initial letter of his name by doing most of it for him and then allowing him to complete it. By this means, one rewards the child for an accomplishment, and this in turn helps to establish the expectancy of this accomplishment.

Establishing an appropriate expectancy for learning is sometimes a matter of "channeling" preexisting motivation in a new direction. A child, for example, may be motivated to become an adult, and therefore to engage in adult activities. An adult-like responsibility, such as tutoring another child, may be an activity in which he participates with enthusiasm. Obviously, he must learn something well before he can engage in tutoring. The teacher can make the tutoring contingent upon his demonstrated mastery of a lesson or subject (cf. Skinner, 1968). The likely result is that he will acquire newly invigorated expectancies for achievement through his own learning.

These and other means can be employed to generate expectancies in learners, and thus to establish new forms of motivation which are not initially present. Additional examples may be found in the book of this series by Baer. It should be emphasized, however, that the acquiring of an expectancy does not itself complete the learning; instead, it simply prepares the way for the learning that is to follow. Establishing motivation is a preparatory phase for an act of learning.

Apprehending Phase

The motivated learner must first receive the stimulation that will, in some transformed way, enter into the essential learning incident and be stored in his memory. He must, in other words, *attend* to the parts of the total stimulation that are relevant to his learning purpose. If he is listening to an oral communication, he must attend to its meaning as a set of sentences, and not to its cadence, accent, or musical quality. If he is reading a textbook, he needs to attend to its propositional meaning, and not to its style of print or arrangement on the page. If he is observing a picture or demonstration, he must attend to the events and objects displayed, but not to their unessential features.

Attending. The process of attention is usually conceived as a temporary internal state, called *mental sets*, or simply a *set* (Hebb, 1972). Once established, a set operates as one kind of executive control process (Figure 1.2). A set to attend may be activated by external stimulation and persist over a limited period of time alerting the individual to receive certain kinds of stimulation. "Listen to the next two words I say, to see if they are different" serves to establish an attentional set. Attention may be initially captured by sudden changes in stimulation, a principle used in advertising displays, and in motion pictures by abrupt "cutting" from one scene to another. In textbooks, attention is caught by varying sizes of type, by interspersing pictures, and by many other means of varying the pattern of stimulation presented. The teacher has available a number of means of influencing attention—changes in intensity of speaking, movements of the arms and head, and many others.

Usually, children in the early grades must learn to direct their attention in response to verbal communications. Although a child may initially attend to a picture shown in a workbook, he must also learn to respond appropriately to such verbal directions as "Look at the upper part of this picture," or "Notice the letter under this picture." Oral or printed directions of this sort may come to control attention over the course of several learning acts. In some instances, however, special efforts need to be made to insure that this early phase of learning—attending—has itself been learned. As the learner gains in experience, the control of his attention by oral or printed directions becomes virtually an automatic feature of his behavior.

Perceiving. The attentional set adopted by the learner

determines what aspects of the external stimulation are *perceived*. (We are now dealing with outputs from the sensory register, Figure 1.2). In other words, the registration of stimuli by the learner is a matter of *selective perception*. Guided by previous learning, by verbal directions, or by other cues, the learner perceives the words on a printed page, not the composition of the print and paper; he perceives the form of a printed triangle, not the thickness of its lines. Given a different attentional set for a different learning goal, he might attend to the type of print rather than to the words, or to the characteristics of the lines rather than the form of the triangle. His perception is selective, as determined by the attentional set which has been adopted, and the set in turn is influenced by directions which reflect the particular goal of learning. Of course, it is common for sophisticated learners to give themselves directions and thus control their own attention processes.

In order for selective perception to be possible, the various features of external stimulation must be distinguished or *discriminated*. Although many discriminations have been learned by the child by the time he attains school age, some may not have been, and this fact establishes the need for *perceptual learning* (Gibson, 1968). For example, the child in kindergarten or first grade may not yet have learned to perceive a printed "d" as different from a printed "b"; they look the same to him. In hearing musical sounds, he may not yet have learned to discriminate the progressions sol-fa and fa-sol. Thus, before further learning can occur, the young child may need to learn to discriminate; that is, he must learn to perceive selectively the features of external stimulation which enter into other acts of learning. (See the volume in this series by Reese).

Acquisition Phase

Once the external situation has been attended to and perceived, the act of learning can proceed. The phase of acquisition includes what we have called the essential incident of learning—the moment in time at which some newly

formed entity is entered into the short-term memory, later
to be further transformed into a "persisting state" in long-
term memory.

Coding. What remains temporarily in the short-term
memory, however, is apparently not the same as what has
been directly perceived. There is a *transformation* of the
perceived entity into a form which is most readily storable.
This important process is called *coding*. The existence of
this process is revealed by studies which show that, generally speaking, what is remembered is almost never
exactly the same as the original stimulation that gave rise
to the learning. The material presented is sometimes dis-
torted in certain ways, sometimes simplified or "regular-
ized," and sometimes embellished. What is stored, as the
result of an act of learning, is apparently not an exact
representation or "mental picture" of what was seen or
heard.

A number of instances of the coding process can be
found in reports on studies of learning. For example, when
individuals in a laboratory experiment were asked to learn
the shapes of simple figures and later asked to draw them,
their reproductions showed a number of kinds of altera-
tions tending to make the figures simpler and more
symmetrical (Gibson, 1929). Two of these figures and
several of their reproductions are shown in Figure 2.2. The
changes in the figures presumably occurred when they
were coded by the learners, each in a somewhat different
way.

Coding for long-term storage. Still other kinds of transformations of material occur when the information enters
long-term memory. In this case, the coding may be said to
serve the purpose of making whatever is learned more
highly memorable. Greater retention may occur when
stimuli are grouped in certain ways, classified under previously learned concepts, or simplified as principles. For
instance, the series 1491625364964 may be coded by a

rule pertaining to squares of numbers, which can readily be seen if the numbers are grouped: 1 4 9 16 25 36 49 . . . (Katona, 1940).

Figure 2.2
Original figures and reproductions of them made by several different learners.

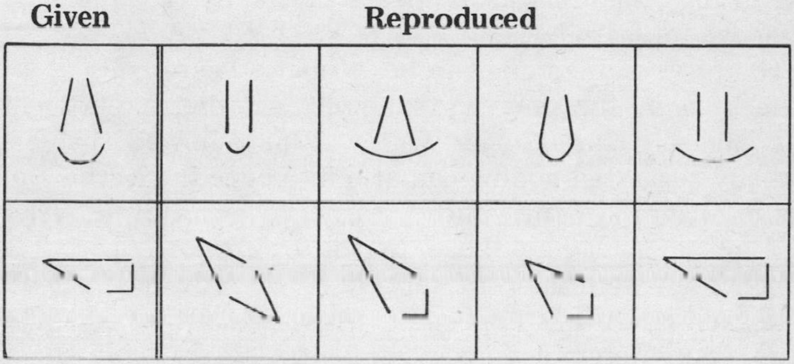

Given   Reproduced

From Gibson, J. J. The reproduction of visually perceived forms. *Journal of Experimental Psychology*, 1929, 12, 1-39. Copyright 1929, American Psychological Association.

An example of coding comes from a study (Rohwer and Lynch, 1966) in which sixth grade children were asked to learn twenty pairs of words (like BEE-DOG, STICK-COW). They first studied the total list, and later were asked to repeat the second word when given the first. For half of the children, the words were presented as part of a sentence containing a verb, as "The STICK hurts the COW." For the other half, the same words were presented as part of a conjunctive phrase, such as "the STICK or the COW." The sentence form was found to be considerably more effective as a means of coding than was the phrase. During two "test-trials," each following a "study-trial," the children who studied the words in sentences recalled the second word correctly 54 percent of the time. Those children who studied the words in phrases, however, recalled correctly only 34 percent of the time. It was known from a previous investigation (Jensen and Rohwer, 1963) that single words can best be learned when embedded in a larger string of words forming a phrase or sentence. This study went on to explore the effectiveness of different *kinds of syntax* as coding devices. Still other studies (e.g., Levin and Kaplan, 1972) have demonstrated that pictures suggesting *visual images* as means of coding can be highly effective for learning.

The process of coding can be influenced externally as we have seen in the previous example. Another experiment (Carmichael, Hogan, and Walter, 1932) showed that externally suggested coding can also influence the learning of figure shapes. In this study, learners were shown twelve different figures like those in the center of Figure 2.3, which they were later to reproduce by drawing. Just before each figure was exposed, the experimenter said, "The next figure resembles eyeglasses" to one set of learners, whereas he said "The next figure resembles a *dumbbell*" to another set of learners; and so on for the remaining figures. The reproductions drawn by the learners clearly indicate the effect of these verbal communications on the coding process.

While it is possible for coding procedures to be suggested externally, it should be borne in mind that the learner may use his own schemes, which may be quite idiosyncratic, and that these often are more effective than others which are supplied for him. In many instances of learning, *encouraging the learner to encode* (i.e., using a coding scheme), in whatever manner he chooses, may be the best procedure.

Retention Phase

The learned entity, somehow altered by the coding process, now enters into the *memory storage* of long-term memory. This is the phase of learning about which we

Figure 2.3
Changes in the reproduction of figures when
their exposure was preceded by suggested
"encodings."

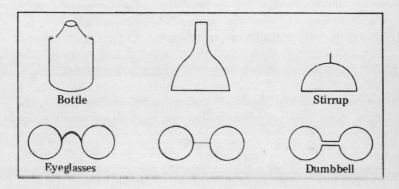

Bottle   Stirrup
Eyeglasses   Dumbbell

Reproduced from Figure 7.20, Gagné and Fleishman, *Psychology
and Human Performance*, copyright Holt, Rinehart & Winston, Inc.,
1959; after Carmichael, Hogan, and Walter, 1932. Reprinted by permission of Holt, Rinehart and Winston, Inc.

perhaps know least, because it is least accessible to investigation. Here are some possibilities concerning its properties:

1. What is learned may be stored in a permanent
fashion, with undiminished intensity over many years, as
though it were stored on permanent magnetic tape. This
possibility is suggested by neurological studies made during
surgical operations on the brain (Adams, 1967). When
small areas of the brain surface are stimulated electrically,
the patient may experience entire scenes of moments in his
past life in rich detail.

2. Some kinds of things that are learned may undergo
very gradual "fading" with the passage of time. This suggestion arises from the known gradual losses of memory

that occur over many years in all of us. An individual may be able to recall fewer and fewer details of what he knows about a childhood friend, for example, even though his name remains memorable as the years go on.

3. Memory storage may be subject to "interference," in the sense that newer memories obscure older ones because they become confused with them (or, less probably, "erase" them). A newly learned telephone number, for example, may initially become confused with a number it has replaced and then apparently block it out entirely. The phenomenon of interference is well known in relation to memory. However, it is by no means certain that this effect occurs in the "memory store" itself—it may instead be something that happens in the retrieval phase (next to be described).

Thus, there are real limits to what is now known about memory storage and its properties. It may have the fundamental characteristic of permanence, or this property may only be partial, applying to some kinds of memories and not to others. One aspect of memory storage that should be emphasized, however, is the fact that the capacity of long-term memory is very great. There is little indication that newly learned entities take the place of previously learned things because there is "no more room." We simply do not know the full extent of this capacity. As exhibited in highly educated people, it seems virtually limitless. No one should imagine that a student's long-term memory can be overloaded.

Recall Phase

In order to qualify as a more-or-less permanent behavior modification, an act of learning must include a phase in which the learned modification is recalled so that it can be exhibited as a performance. The process at work during this phase is called *retrieval*. Somehow, the memory store is searched and the learned entity revivified. What has been stored becomes "accessible." The process is presumably at work even for learning which has occurred a few minutes previously. To be sure, however, there may be differences in the strategies of retrieval for recent and for longer-term memories.

Retrieval. As is true for most other processes of learning, the process of retrieval may be affected by external stimulation. Cues for retrieval may be suggested by verbal communications to the learner. For example, in "jogging the memory" of a student who is trying to recall what specific gravity means, one might say "do you remember Archimedes?"

Sometimes, the external cue takes the form of reminding the learner of his previous encoding, as in the following example (Tulving and Pearlstone, 1966). High school students were asked to learn lists of words belonging to certain categories (four-footed animals, weapons, professions, etc.) The words themselves, corresponding to these categories, were such as *cow, rat; bomb, cannon; engineer, lawyer.* They were randomly arranged in lists of three different lengths, containing twelve, twenty-four, or forty-eight words. Learners were given the task of learning and remembering the words in the list. The words were read, and each was preceded by a category word, which the learners were told did not have to be remembered. Later, one group of learners recalled the words by being given "cues" for the categories, while another group was not given these cues. For the short lists of twelve words, providing cues made little difference in recall. For the forty-eight word lists, however, the category cues made a very large difference, on the average 74 percent (for the cued condition) to 32 percent (for those not cued). These results, then, show previously learned categories can function as cues to the retrieval of otherwise unrelated words. Retrieval cues appear to be most effective when they are introduced at the time learning first occurs.

Again, as in the case of coding, it must be remembered that the sophisticated learner supplies his own retrieval cues. As we shall see in the next chapter, an important goal of school learning is the development of an *independent* learner. Although it is important for the design of instruction to make suitable provision for external activation of the retrieval process, it is even more important for the learner to acquire strategies that enable him to do this himself. In order to encourage such development, however, a teacher needs to know "what is going on" in learning, and thereby to choose judiciously the communications he makes to the student.

Generalization Phase

Retrieval of what is learned does not always occur in the same situation or within the same *context* that surrounded the original learning. After all, one expects the student learner to be able to use the principle of a lever in moving heavy objects in real life, not simply in the context of his science textbook. In other words, there must be *generalization* of the learning that has occurred. The recall of what has been learned and its application to new and different contexts is referred to as the *transfer of learning*, often shortened to *transfer*.

An example of transfer.   A famous study on transfer was performed many years ago (Judd, 1908) and redone later by Hendrickson and Schroeder (1941). Three groups of junior high school boys, chosen to be roughly equal in age and intelligence, were given the task of hitting a target submerged under water by shooting at it with an air rifle. They practiced shooting at a target six inches below the surface. One group simply practiced until they got three consecutive hits. A second group was given a general explanation of the principles of refraction, using a diagram of a rock in a lake, before they practiced. The third group received the same explanation and also a working rule "The deeper the lake is, the farther the real rock will be from the image rock," followed by practice. Transfer of learning was assessed by the boys' performance in hitting a second target, this time at a depth of two inches. It was found that the third group, which had received both the explanation and a working rule, showed the greatest amount of transfer of learning to this second task. The "working rule" was apparently the most important factor in producing transfer.

We can assume that the boys who participated in this study learned how to aim at a submerged target as a result of their practice with the one six inches below the surface. In order to transfer this experience to the situation involving the second target, however, they needed a rule for changing aim with a change in degree of submersion. Those boys who learned about refraction presumably learned this principle in some form. It is particularly significant, though that the group evidencing the greatest transfer learned a practical rule that could be directly applied to the new situation. Thus, this study suggests that "understanding the principles" in a general sense, while important to transfer, may not always be sufficient. It may be that the "working rule" was more directly related to the new situation, or that it functioned as a retrieval cue to connect the principles to the new context (cf. Haselrud, 1973).

Transfer in school learning.   Since transfer is so obviously a goal of school learning, instruction needs to include the means of insuring retrieval in the greatest variety of contexts possible. "Teaching for transfer" may be interpreted as aiming to provide the learner with processes for retrieval that will apply in many kinds of practical contexts. Variety of contexts for learning thus becomes one of the important conditions supporting the transfer phase of the learning process. A further discussion of instructional techniques used to enhance transfer occurs in Chapter 4.

Performance Phase

The performance phase of learning seems fairly straightforward. The response generator (Figure 1.2) organizes the learner's responses and allows him to exhibit a performance that reflects what he has learned.

For the learner, the performance made possible by the act of learning serves the important function of preparing the way for feedback, which is the next phase. Although the learner may in some instances think that he "has it," the actual performance is the best way for him to assure himself that learning has occurred. By this means, he obtains the satisfaction that comes from perceiving the product of his learning. The student of science who has "learned how" to make a graph of the growth of a plant proceeds without hesitation to respond by constructing such a graph.

The learner's performance. The performance of the learner has an essential function for the observer or for the teacher. This product of responding verifies that learning has taken place—that behavior has indeed been modified. The child who previously could not dependably distinguish the sounds of *a* in printed words like *mat* and *mate* now does so. The student who previously could not express 9/27 as .333 now exhibits this kind of performance unhesitatingly. The youngster who was previously unable to write a sentence using "whom" correctly now shows by his performance that he can. There is, of course, the question of how many instances of performance are required as convincing verification that learning has occurred. No simple answer can be given to this question, since it depends on the degree of generality of the performance itself. Usually, a single instance of performance is not entirely convincing; the student may have "stumbled on" a correct performance. If the performance is displayed in two different examples, the inference that learning has occurred is distinctly better, and three makes the conclusion quite firm. However, it may be noted that, in the give-and-take of the classroom, the single instance of performance often suffices as evidence of learning.

Feedback Phase

Once the learner has exhibited the new performance made

possible by learning, he at once perceives that he has achieved the anticipated goal. This "informational feedback" is what many learning theorists consider the essence of the process called *reinforcement*. This process is of widespread significance to human behavior, particularly to human learning (Krasner and Ullman, 1965; Skinner, 1968; see also the volume by Baer in this series). It is important to note that, according to this conception, reinforcement "works" in human learning because the expectancy established during the motivational phase of learning is now confirmed during the feedback phase. Presumably, the process of reinforcement operates in the human being not because a reward is actually provided, but because an *anticipation of reward is confirmed*. The importance of the motivational phase to the act of learning is again reemphasized by the reinforcement process. The "learning loop" is closed by reinforcement. The state of expectancy established during the motivational phase results in feedback that confirms this expectancy.

The feedback phase of learning may obviously be influenced by events external to the learner. Sometimes, the feedback is "naturally" provided by the learner's performance itself, for example, the event of a basketball going through the hoop or the balance in a science exercise coming to equilibrium. On other occasions, the learner must make some verifying response to obtain suitable feedback, as when he checks the "balance" of a chemical or algebraic equation. Often, too, the informative feedback is obtained by comparison with a standard. The child may compare his printed *H* with a standard in a model book; the student's pronunciation of a German "ch" may be compared with feedback from the teacher or from an audio tape. The *informational* nature of the feedback appears to be its most critical feature, so far as the support of learning is concerned (Estes, 1972).

Learning in Relation to Instruction

A total act of learning may be conceived as a series of

events which often has as short a duration as a few seconds. The phases of this series of events begin with the establishment of motivation and proceed through apprehending, acquisition (the essential learning incident), retention, recall, generalization, performance, and feedback. Systematic studies of these various learning events have led to the development of models of learning as a set of internal processes corresponding to learning phases. For each phase of learning, there is conceived to be one or more *internal processes* in the learner's central nervous system, which transform the information from one form to another until the individual responds in a performance.

The internal processes of learning may be influenced by *external* events—stimuli from the learner's environment, which often are verbal communications from a teacher, a textbook, or some other source. These external events, when they are planned for the purpose of supporting learning, are called by the general name of *instruction*. As the manager of instruction, it is the teacher's job to plan, design, select, and supervise the arrangement of these external events, with the aim of activating the necessary learning processes. Of course, there are instances in which few of these external influences are necessary—the learner may be self-motivated and able to carry out the various additional actions needed for self-instruction. Self-instruction, however, does not provide a dependable model for learning, as it is not applicable to all circumstances of school learning. Instruction is best planned so that it will always make available the external stimulation needed to support the internal processes of learning. The learner who can instruct himself finds it possible to ignore these external influences or perhaps to refer to them occasionally. However, learners will find instruction helpful for attaining their goals in many situations.

Learning processes and external events. A summary of learning processes and the general nature of external events which may be brought to bear upon them is given in

Table 2.1. The information in this table provides a review of the discussion in this chapter, as well as a preview of material in later chapters dealing with instructional planning.

Table 2.1
Processes of Learning and the Influence of External Events

Learning Phase	Process	Influencing External Events
Motivation	Expectancy	1. Communicating the goal to be achieved; or 2. Prior confirmation of expectancy through successful experience
Apprehending	Attention; Selective Perception	1. Change in stimulation to activate attention; 2. Prior perceptual learning; or 3. Added differential cues for perception
Acquisition	Coding; Storage Entry	Suggested schemes for coding
Retention	Storage	Not known
Recall	Retrieval	1. Suggested schemes for retrieval; 2. Cues for retrieval
Generalization	Transfer	Variety of contexts for retrieval cueing
Performance	Responding	Instances of the performance ("examples")
Feedback	Reinforcement	Informational feedback providing verification or comparison with a standard

An outline of the kinds of external events that constitute instruction is provided in the final column of Table 2.1, opposite the learning process to which they apply. For example, for the motivation phase of learning, the table indicates that the process of *expectancy* may be established by (1) communicating to the learner what he will be able to accomplish when learning has been completed, or (2) insuring that the learner has previously had a "success" experience in the performance he is about to learn. Similar references are made to the events that can be used to support each of the other processes in the total learning act, insofar as these are known. This information outlines the main points of our discussion of external influences on the learning processes.

We shall have more to say later about instruction, but its major purposes and the outlines of its structure are suggested by the contents of Table 2.1. If a designer of instruction (or a teacher) is concerned with supporting the process of selective perception, for example, he may either depend on prior perceptual learning or provide added cues (pointing, underlining, etc.), which serve to differentiate the stimuli being presented. If concerned with acquisition, the instructor may suggest schemes that aid the coding process, and so on. The sum total of these external events, designed to be appropriate to any given learning goal, becomes the substance of instruction.

The events we have described, both internal and external, are the *general* characteristics of an act of learning. Still other attributes of learning, which must be understood before successful instruction can be designed in any area of the school curriculum, are those features that are *specific* to different kinds of learned performances, or, to use the terms we shall employ, to different types of *learning outcomes*. This topic will be discussed in the next chapter.

General References

Theories of Learning

Hilgard, E. R., & Bower, G. H. *Theories of learning.* (4th ed.) New York: Appleton-Century-Crofts, 1974.

Hill, W. F. *Learning: A survey of psychological interpretations.* San Francisco: Chandler, 1963.

Learning Processes

Adams, J. A. *Human memory.* New York: McGraw-Hill, 1967.

Deese, J. & Hulse, S. H. *Psychology of learning.* (3rd ed.) New York: McGraw-Hill, 1967.

Kimble, G. A. *Hilgard and Marquis' conditioning and learning.* (2nd ed.) New York: Appleton-Century-Crofts, 1961.

Travers, R. M. W. *Essentials of learning* (3rd ed.) New York: Macmillan, 1972.

Learning and Instruction

Gagné, R. M., & Briggs, L. J. *Principles of instructional design.* New York: Holt, Rinehart & Winston, 1974.

Stephens, J. M., & Evans, E. D. *Development and classroom learning: An introduction to educational psychology.* New York: Holt, Rinehart & Winston, 1973.

Chapter 3 The Outcomes of Learning

Learning is activated by a variety of kinds of stimulation from the learner's environment. This stimulation is the *input* to the processes of learning. Their *output*, as we have seen in Chapter 2, is a modification of behavior that is observed as human performance. The kinds of performance that are seen as evidence of learning in educational programs are many and varied. They range from relatively simple productions like line drawing and syllable pronunciation in the young child to the most complex varieties of problem solution in adolescents and adults. They occur in all the many content areas of school curriculum and adult education programs.

Despite the great diversity of human performances that result from learning, it is possible to classify these performances in such a way as to draw useful implications from them that can improve our understanding of the learning process. To do this, we must first recall that learning establishes *persisting states* in the learner (as discussed in Chapter 1). These states make possible the performances that are observed. Although the performances themselves vary in many dimensions, the underlying states may be classified as having certain formal properties in common. We choose here to call these persisting states *capabilities*, a word which implies that they make the individual *capable* of certain performances.

Incidentally, various terms often have approximately the same meaning as *capability*, although there may be shades of difference. Some of these terms are *ability*, *competency*, and (for such learned states as attitudes) *dispositions*. In addition, there is the word *capacity*, which traditionally has a different meaning, namely, the innate limit of what an individual can learn. According to this usage, an individual may have the *capacity* for learning certain *capabilities*; but what he learns are the *capabilities*. The term capabilities will be used consistently throughout this book.

The outcomes of learning, then, are human capabilities which make possible a variety of performances. We can now proceed to consider the questions: What kinds of human capabilities are there? What sorts of categories of these capabilities can be described that have common properties?

Types of Learned Capabilities

Certain kinds of learning outcomes resemble each other, even though they may occur in different fields or deal with different subject matter. For example, the learner may acquire a "fact" in the field of American history ("Opposition to a tax on tea led to the Boston Tea Party"); or in science ("Oxygen was identified as a chemical element by Lavoisier"); or in music ("Beethoven composed nine symphonies"). The capability being learned in each case is being able to *state* the fact. The occurrence of these facts in different fields of organized knowledge does not prevent their being classified as the same general kind of learned capability.

The similarities in other kinds of capabilities drawn from different fields may not be so immediately obvious, but nevertheless they are equally compelling. A learner of his native language may have learned to perform certain "operations" on sentences, such as converting an active sentence to a passive form (as in changing "The boy held the dog on a leash" to "The dog was held on a leash by the boy"). In quite a different field, mathematics, the same learner may have acquired the capability of performing "operations" on equations (as in changing $a + b - c = 0$ to $a + b = c$). Although the subject matter is quite different and the essential logic of the operations also quite different, there are nevertheless common features to these two kinds of performance. The most important common characteristic is that the capability in both cases, assuming it has been fully learned, can be exhibited with *any* sentence of the same class or with *any* equation of the same type. It is, in other words, *rule-following* behavior, whether the subject matter is language or mathematics.

These examples are perhaps sufficient to introduce the idea that types of human capabilities can be identified as categories that cut across subject matter fields, and indeed are independent of them, so far as their formal characteristics are concerned. Different types of capabilities occur *within* particular fields of study, as well as *across* various fields of the curriculum. Distinguishing the types of human capabilities, considered as learning outcomes, makes possible a refined understanding of the learning process and thus permits the drawing of relatively precise implications for the design of instruction.

There are five major categories of learning outcomes— that is, five classes of learned human capabilities (Gagné, 1972). In the order in which we shall consider them here (which implies no particular order of complexity or importance), they are (1) *verbal information*, (2) *intellectual skills*, (3) *cognitive strategies*, (4) *attitudes*, and (5) *motor skills*. The following sections of this chapter describe the major characteristics of these categories, insofar as they are known at present. It will be apparent that a greater amount of systematic knowledge is available about some of these categories than about others. However, the distinctions among them are quite adequate to make their differential properties dependably clear.

Verbal Information

All of us acquire large amounts of verbal information during our lifetimes. A great deal of such information is acquired in school or other organized educational programs. Much information is acquired by word of mouth, from reading, and from radio and television. The units of information acquired can be classified as "facts," "names," "principles," and "generalizations." Verbal information is man's primary method of transmitting accumulated knowledge to successive generations—knowledge about the world and its peoples, about historical events and trends, about the culture of a civilization as represented in its literature and art, and about current and practical affairs of life.

Information is often learned by means of verbal communications presented to the learner in oral or printed form. Alternatively, the learner may first state the information to himself as a proposition. For example, when the learner acquires information about a picture, he might "say to himself" that there are oak trees in the foreground. However it is presented, learning the information involves coding it. That is to say, the information is incorporated into some more comprehensive meaningful complex which is already present in the learner's memory.

The learning of verbal information as a capability means that the individual is able to *state* in propositional form what he has learned. He can say, or write, or otherwise represent the information he has learned as a *sentence* (proposition). Strictly speaking, the learner who is able to repeat the words HOUSE-BOTTLE-MOUNTAIN in the proper order may have learned something, but he has not learned information. In contrast, the individual who can verbally state POLICE ARREST BURGLARS *has* acquired information. What makes the latter information is its sentence form. Even the smallest type of informational unit, a name or label, carries with it the implied sentence form, as in (THIS IS A) HOUSE. The unit of information, then, is a sentence that can be verbally stated, even if part of the sentence is merely implied or "understood." To define verbal information as a statable sentence does not necessarily mean that it is stored that way in memory. Apparently, information can be stored as a visual image or some other kind of image. The retrieval of information may also be cued by other than verbal means, as when a picture or diagram is used to remind the learner of information he has previously learned. But what the learner is able to *do*, when he has learned information, is to *state* it. Of course, he may state it "in his own words," rather than in verbatim form.

Organized bodies of information, the words of which have meaning for the learner, are usually referred to as *knowledge*. Since learner acquisition of knowledge of various sorts is a generally accepted educational goal, learning conditions must be designed to support the learning of information and also the learning of meanings (concepts). We shall deal with the learning of concepts in the next section.

The functions of information and knowledge. Information, particularly when it occurs as organized knowledge, has a number of useful functions for the student. First, it often serves as a necessary prerequisite for further learning. For example, the student who is learning basic principles of weather prediction needs information about clouds, winds, temperature ranges, and terrain features, among other things. The student must learn these various items of information so that he can later incorporate them into the complex rules of weather prediction. A lesson or text customarily presents the necessary items of information first, before explaining how weather prediction is done. Alternatively, a text chapter on weather prediction methods may contain an initial section that reviews previously learned information.

Some kinds of information are of practical importance to the individual during his entire lifetime. These include the names of common objects, the days of the week, the months of the year, and many other "labels" required for everyday communication. The individual also retains and uses information about locations, for example, the cities and states in his country and the countries, oceans, and continents of the world. He may and usually does have basic information about certain jobs and professions, such as teacher, lawyer, physician, and so on. The amount and kind of such practically useful information learned by the individual depends on his inclinations, which in turn are often influenced by his manner of living. Obviously, the school attempts to provide at least the minimum essentials of practical information for all students.

A third function of knowledge is a very important one, although the means of its operation are as yet poorly understood. Organized and associated bodies of knowledge are believed to provide a *vehicle for thought*. When an individual tries to solve a novel problem, he "thinks of" many things in his search for a tentative solution. At this stage in his thinking, he is not employing logic—that will come later. Instead, he is conducting a search among the various items of information, both organized and scattered, available to him in his memory. Using organized information, for example, the individual may relate the effects of the interest rate on the prices of goods to the effects of a speed-governor on a steam engine. This thought may then become a key idea in the solution of a problem (for the student). The enormous store of information which most of us possess provides almost limitless possibilities for flexible thinking.

Intellectual Skills

A second important category of learned capabilities is intellectual skills (Gagné, 1970). Simply stated, these consti-tute *knowing how*, as contrasted with the *knowing that* of information. The student learns *how* to transform printed symbols on a page into recognizable words; *how* to convert fractions to decimals; *how* to make verbs agree with sub-jects of sentences; *how* to turn a French statement into a question; *how* to relate the force acting upon a body to its mass and acceleration. It would not be possible to learn all these things as information, or as facts, because too many individual instances exist. The intellectual skills a student learns enable him to respond adequately to entire *classes* (that is, groups or categories) of natural phenomena. These skills are ways the learner acquires of interacting with his environment through *symbols*. The symbols he uses in-clude letters, numerals, words, and pictorial diagrams of many kinds.

Intellectual skills may be divided into several subcate-gories, and these subcategories can be ordered according to the complexity of mental operation they imply. Further-more, they are related to each other in that the more complex skills require the prior learning of simpler skills. The names of these intellectual skills and their ordering are shown in Figure 3.1. Beginning with the simplest, they are *discriminations*, *concepts*, *rules*, and *higher-order rules*. (Actually, there are even simpler learned entities, but we need not be concerned with them in this volume. See Gagné, 1970.) Learning each of these types of skills de-pends on the prior learning of one or more of the next simpler types of skills as *prerequisites*. It will be most use-ful to describe the nature of these learned skills by begin-ning with the simplest.

Discriminations. In responding to his environment via symbols, the learner must first acquire the simple skill of distinguishing one feature of an object from another, which includes distinguishing one symbol from another. Many commonly useful discriminations are of course learned in early childhood, often without deliberate intent.

The infant learns gross discriminations pertaining to the features of his environment—colors, shapes, and sounds—before he learns to speak. These discriminations continue to increase in the fineness of detail to which they refer as the child gains experience (Gibson, 1968).

Figure 3.1
Varieties of intellectual skills, arranged (bottom to top) in order of increasing complexity (Gagné, 1970).

HIGHER-ORDER RULES

require as prerequisites

RULES

require as prerequisites

CONCEPTS

require as prerequisites

DISCRIMINATIONS

require as prerequisites

(simple types of learning)

By the time the individual begins to attend school, he

has already learned a great many important and useful discriminations, but some have not yet been acquired. Thus, early education is often concerned with the learning of finer discriminations of shapes, textures, sounds, and other kinds of stimulation. Examples are the discrimination of letter forms, like m and n, or of the sounds of letters such as v and b. Discrimination learning, it may be noted, is simply another name for the "perceptual learning" mentioned in the previous chapter. When completed, it results in the *selective perception* of features of the learner's environment. The learning of discriminations is of course not confined to the early years of life. Beyond the early grades, the student may need to acquire discriminations of newly encountered symbols like $\geqslant$ and $\leqslant$, new foreign-word sounds, or new visual fields such as are seen through microscopes.

A learned discrimination is the capability of *distinguishing* one feature of stimulation from another or one symbol from another. The child who initially doesn't "see the difference" between a printed d and a printed b acquires the discimination, and now sees these symbols as different. He may learn a discrimination which enables him to distinguish a figure like ◻ from a figure like ◿, or a set of objects like :. from a set like :: . It should be carefully noted, however, that a discrimination makes it possible for the learner only to *tell the difference* among stimuli—not to name them or use them in some other way. Acquiring a discrimination merely enables the child, for example, to *respond differently* to d and b, not to name them as "d" and "b." Of course, he must be able to do the first (discriminate) before he can do the second (name). Thus, learning discriminations is important mainly because it is a necessary prerequisite to other learning.

Concepts.   When the prerequisite discriminations are available to the learner, he is then able to learn *concepts*. The simplest form of concepts are *concrete concepts*, which are *classes* of object qualities, objects, and events. Again, many concrete concepts are learned in early childhood, but new concepts may be learned at any time during a person's lifetime. For example, the young child learns a number of concrete concepts identifying objects in his environment, such as chair, table, floor, ceiling, door, road, tree, (his) mother, (his) father, dog, fish, and so on. He also learns concepts of object qualities, such as color, round, square, pointed, soft, hard, smooth, and many others. Some concrete concepts are relational, such as up, down, outside, inside, far, near.

When the child begins his schooling, he may already have acquired quite a number of concrete concepts, which enable him to identify single instances of classes of objects and object-qualities in his environment. He may not yet know some classes of things and events—for example, the concepts "rectangular," "jagged," or "branch." Particularly important among concrete concepts to be learned in early education are relational concepts such as "right," "left," "middle," "above," "below," "underneath," "behind," and so on. Of course, many concrete concepts are learned throughout formal education and at various times during the individual's life—"cornice," "membrane," "penultimate," for example.

The learned capability called concrete concept enables the individual to *identify* a class of objects, object-qualities, or relations by "pointing out" one or more instances of the class. The "pointing out" may be done in various ways, such as by pointing, or marking or circling with a pencil, by physically separating instances and noninstances, or whatever; the manner of responding is not important. What is important is that the acquisition of a concrete concept enables the learner to identify (to himself, or to another person) the entire class of things by indicating one or more examples of the class.

Often, the capability of identifying a concrete concept is shown by naming. It is typical, for example, to determine whether an individual has acquired a particular concrete concept by asking him to name it, or alternatively by using its class name in asking him to identify it. Thus, one may ask the child, to "show me the elephant" in a picture containing several animals; or to "show me which is the middle one" in a group of objects. But the use of names in these cases is an incidental feature of the concrete concept, not an essential one. Learning a name or a "label" is not in itself the criterion of learning a concept and in fact is quite distinct from it. A learner may be able to identify a class of object-qualities, for example, five-sidedness, without knowing the term pentagon. The converse is also obviously true—a learner may be able to make the verbal response "pentagon" without being able to identify instances of pentagonal shapes. Having the capability of a concrete concept means "knowing the meaning" of a name or label; which is to say, being able to identify the class by means of its particular instances.

Defined concepts. Some concepts of objects, object-qualities, and relations cannot be identified by "pointing them out." They must instead be *defined*. This means that one must use a sentence (or proposition) to identify a class of things. A simple example is an "obstacle," whose meaning must be communicated by a sentence such as "an obstacle is something that stands in the way." Since many kinds of things might serve as obstacles, it would not be possible to identify the entire class of the concept "obstacle" by pointing to a few examples; accordingly, this very general class must be identified by means of a definition. Another example is "pivot," which must be defined by the sentence "an object rests or turns on the pointed end of a shaft (a pivot)." Relational concepts also must often be defined, rather than directly "pointed out," as in the case of "uncle," "suburb," and "sell." Obviously, the learning that takes place in schools is filled with defined concepts.

Concrete concepts can, of course, be replaced or given added meaning by defined concepts, and often this is a major aim of an educational topic. Concepts like "two" and "three" are originally concrete concepts for the young child, which are simply identified by him (as by pointing) without the use of a definition. These concepts may be replaced in school learning by defined concepts in which three becomes "a set formed by joining the set one to the set two." Similarly, the concrete concept of "circle," as something which can be pointed to, may be augmented in school learning by the defined concept "the locus of points in a plane equidistant from a point." The concretely identifiable "flower" becomes by definition "the part of a seed plant containing the reproductive organs and their envelopes." Obviously, for many purposes, individuals continue to employ the concrete concept as a means for communication; few carpenters would be able to define a circle, and few poets a flower.

The learner has acquired a defined concept when he can *demonstrate*, or show how to use, the definition. In doing this, he is *classifying* instances of the concept. If he has learned the concept "longitude," for example, he must be able to show how to use the definition "angular distance east or west on the earth's surface." This means that he must identify the component concepts "angular distance," "east-west," and "earth's surface," and, having done this, show how these concepts are related by a rule which classifies the *longitude* of places. Note that it is not necessary for the learner to *state* the definition in order to demonstrate that he knows the concept. As a minimum, all he must do is show how he can obtain a measure of east-west distance called longitude. In effect, he knows the concept when he is given a globe and can perform correctly in response to the directions: "Suppose I were located at the zero point on the earth's surface. Show how I would find the longitude of this other point." It is often convenient, however, for the learner to demonstrate his learning of a defined concept by using words to refer to its components.

The defined concept, then, is in actuality a classifying rule. It is therefore simply a special case of the type of intellectual skill called *rule*, which will be next described.

Rules.   A widely occurring kind of intellectual skill is called a *rule*. It is common to think of a rule as a verbal statement, such as "one inch equals 2.54 centimeters." But the statement of a rule is merely the representation of it—the rule itself is a learned capability of an individual learner. We say that a learner has learned a rule when he can "follow it" in his performances. In other words, a rule is a learned capability which makes it possible for the individual to *do* something, using symbols (most commonly, the symbols of language and mathematics). The capability of doing something must be carefully distinguished from *stating* something, which is the information capability previously described.

A great deal of learning within education programs is concerned with rules. The young child learns rules which enable him to "decode" words in reading, to spell words, to compose sentences, to perform arithmetic computations, and to derive mathematical equivalencies. The older student learns rules which enable him to find physical relations of mass, time, and distance, to balance chemical equations, to apply the laws of genetic inheritance, to compose paragraphs, themes, and stories, and to carry out many other kinds of performances. A college student or other adult also learns a host of rules—the structure of poetry, the rules of music composition, the construction of foreign language communications, and many others. All these kinds of learning involve the use of symbols to represent and interact with the learner's environment in *generalized* ways. Their learning makes it possible for the learner to exhibit rule-governed behavior.

Rules as learned capabilities make it possible for the individual to respond to a *class* of things with a *class* of performances. Thus, in forming a word (adverb) to modify an adjective, the learner can apply the rule of adding "ly" and write "joyful*ly* busy" rather than "joyful busy." Furthermore, he is able to recognize at once that almost every adjective modifier must have an added suffix, usually "ly." Rather than learning an adverbial form for every adjective in the language, he applies a *rule* to an entire class of words. Perhaps the learner has just encountered an adjective like "hypothetical"; it is readily possible, applying a learned rule, to form the adverb "hypothetically," even though he may never have seen it before. In this way his competence is enormously extended.

Higher-order rules. Sometimes, more complex rules are "put together" by the learner by combining simpler ones. Usually, when this happens, the learner is engaged in solving a novel problem. The higher-order rule which results is verified in the usual way—by means of a performance which applies it to the problem at hand and perhaps to other instances of a similar sort. It is still a rule and differs only in complexity from the simpler rules which compose it.

Suppose, for example, that the learner is tackling the problem, for the first time in his life, of finding the area of a four-sided figure like that shown in Figure 3.2, given the information included there. In order to do this, he must apply a number of simpler rules, such as the rule for finding the area of a rectangle, the rule for identity of right triangles, and others. Solving the problem requires putting these together to arrive at a higher-order rule that is applicable to all such figures, whatever their dimensions. Of course, these subordinate rules are not all that is involved in the thinking process, but they are prerequisites to attaining the higher-order rule.

Examples of higher-order rules in mathematics tend to be neat and unambiguous. However, the process of problem-solving is presumably much the same whatever the field of study. Higher-order rules may be derived by the learner in undertaking problems in writing paragraphs, speaking a foreign language, using scientific principles, and applying laws to situations of social or economic conflict. In every case, simpler rules (including defined concepts) are combined into the higher-order rule or rules which then find their application to the problem being addressed. The simpler subordinate rules are clearly prerequisites to the thinking which is demanded.

Figure 3.2
Solving the problem of finding the area of a
regular four-sided figure utilizes subordinate
rules and results in a higher-order rule.

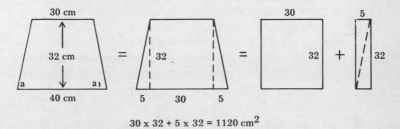

$$30 \times 32 + 5 \times 32 = 1120 \text{ cm}^2$$

SUBORDINATE RULES
> Area of rectangle
> Identity of right triangles
> Division of rectangle into two equal triangles by diagonal
> Multiplying
> Adding

HIGHER-ORDER RULE
> Divide figure into rectangle and triangles; combine identical
> right triangles into rectangle; find areas of rectangles and add.

Summary of intellectual skills. The types of intellectual
skills we have described are learned capabilities which enable the learner to *do* various things by means of symbolic
representations of his environment. Perhaps the best general word to denote the kind of capabilities that intellectual skills imply is *demonstrating*. If the individual has
learned an intellectual skill, he can *demonstrate* its applicability to one or more particular instances of the class of
phenomena to which it refers.

Intellectual skills vary in complexity from discriminations, to concrete concepts, to defined concepts and rules,
and to higher-order rules. They also *build upon* each other,
in the sense that simpler ones are prerequisites for the

more complex skills. This ordered character of intellectual skills has definite implications for their learning, as we shall see in the next chapter.

Cognitive Strategies

Cognitive strategies are internally organized capabilities which the learner makes use of in guiding his own attending, learning, remembering, and thinking. As pointed out in Chapter 1, these capabilities make possible *executive control*. (In Figure 1.2, these are the processes that activate and modify other learning processes.) Their nature can perhaps best be illustrated by contrasting them with intellectual skills. Intellectual skills are oriented toward aspects of the learner's environment; they enable him to deal with numbers, words, and symbols which are "out there." In contrast, cognitive strategies govern the *learner's own behavior* in dealing with his environment; they are, in a sense, "in there." The learner uses a cognitive strategy in attending to various features of what he is reading; *what* he learns may be an intellectual skill or information. He uses a cognitive strategy to select and use a "code" for what he learns, and another strategy for retrieving it. Most importantly, he uses cognitive strategies in thinking about what he has learned and in solving problems. Cognitive strategies are ways the learner has of *managing* the processes of learning (as well as retention and thinking).

Obviously, cognitive strategies are of great importance as learning goals in educational systems. To the extent that strategies of attending, coding, retrieving, transfer, and problem solving can be learned and improved by formal educational means, the learner will increasingly become a *self-learner* and an *independent thinker*. Of course, there will be individual differences in the capacity to learn these valuable capabilities. Nevertheless, it has seemed to most educational scholars eminently worthwhile to provide every student with opportunities for learning cognitive strategies.

When a novel problem is posed for a learner, he must bring to bear upon it the retained effects of prior learning in the form of previously learned information and intellectual skills. Although these capabilities are necessary, they are not sufficient. In addition, the learner must have a *strategy* of approach to the new problem—or possibly he may choose among several alternative strategies. These internally organized strategies enable him to manage his own thinking processes. The originality and soundness of his thinking will be determined in large degree by the appropriateness and efficiency of his cognitive strategies. Many of the implications of cognitive strategies for educational planning are discussed by Bruner (1971).

Emphasis is frequently given in educational writings to the desirability of cognitive strategies as educational outcomes. For example, "learning to learn" and "learning how to think" are often cited as educational goals of high priority. At the same time, it is not evident that there has been a substantial commitment to instruction having these aims in the schools. (Some of the problems involved in designing instruction to support the learning of cognitive strategies are discussed in the next chapter. For an account of some experimental studies, see the volume in this series by Reese.)

Attitudes

Attitudes represent another distinct class of learning outcomes. Many kinds of attitudes can be identified as desirable educational goals. It is hoped, for example, that children will acquire attitudes affecting their social interactions, such as tolerance for racial and ethnic differences, kindness to others, helpfulness, thoughtfulness of others' feelings. (For a further discussion, see the Covington volume in this series.) Attitudes of this sort may initially be acquired in the home, or they may best be learned in social situations involving other children. A second general class of attitudes consists of positive preferences for certain kinds of activities, like listening to music, reading, using mathematics, engaging in physical exercise, or even more generally, a liking for learning itself. A third general class of attitudes pertains to citizenship—a love of country, a concern for societal needs and goals, a willingness to undertake the responsibilities of citizenship. These three major classes merely serve to suggest the range of desirable attitudes and do not exhaust the possibilities. As learned capabilities, attitudes are sometimes coupled in thought with *values.* The latter are generally considered to be more general, whereas attitudes are more specifically oriented toward particular preferences. Attitudes are also referred to as the *affective domain* (Krathwohl, Bloom, & Masia, 1964), a phrase which emphasizes their emotional component. It is questionable, however, whether the "feeling" character of attitudes should be emphasized to the exclusion of their cognitive and behavioral aspects. In particular, it seems unduly restrictive to consider the learning of attitudes as being a matter of "training the emotions." Our consideration of attitudes as learned capabilities has a behavioral emphasis, in the sense that attitudes affect human performances.

An attitude is *an acquired internal state that influences the choice of personal action* towards some class of things, persons, or events. An attitude toward the disposal of personal trash, for example, will influence the choices the individual makes in disposing of gum wrappers, soda cans, food containers, and so on. An attitude toward classical music will influence the choices a person makes in selecting recordings to listen to, concerts to attend, and similar choices. An attitude toward learning about science will influence the choices of newspaper accounts to be read, books to be purchased or borrowed, and television programs to be watched. Obviously, attitudes vary in their "strength" or intensity and also in their direction—one may have a positive attitude toward reading modern fiction or a negative one. Although school education is mainly concerned with the establishment of positive attitudes, attention is also given to certain negative ones, such as the avoidance of harmful drugs or exposure to disease.

Motor Skills

Motor skills, although not the most prominent part of educational goals, are a distinct type of learning outcome and must surely be included as essential components of the individual's repertory of learned capabilities. These skills are learned in connection with such common human activities as driving a car, operating a typewriter, and playing a musical instrument. Motor skills of many particular sorts are involved in athletic and sports activities, as well as a number of occupations such as carpentry, auto repair, machine operation, and many others. In addition, acquiring motor skills is sometimes essential to basic subjects of the school curriculum. Young children learn the skills of printing and writing letters; older students learn new skills of pronouncing sounds of foreign language; science students often need to learn manual skills required in using equipment.

The function of motor skills as learned capabilities is readily evident. They make possible the precise, smooth, and accurately timed execution of performances involving the use of muscles. For example, the activity of driving an automobile requires, at various times, the use of such motor skills as: (1) moving the car at minimal speed while turning; (2) backing at minimal speed, maintaining an angular direction; (3) following the road at driving speeds; (4) accelerating from a stop, and a number of others. As a total activity, driving a car involves several kinds of capabilities, including intellectual skills, information, and attitudes. Even so, it is critical that precisely timed motor performances be learned as motor skills, because they must be available to the driver when he needs them.

Human Capabilities as Learning Outcomes

The five major categories of learned capabilities have now been described—verbal information, intellectual skills, cognitive strategies, attitudes, and motor skills. These represent categories of *what is learned*. How they are learned is the topic of Chapter 4.

Table 3.1 provides a review of the main points of our description of these learned human capabilities. Each of

Table 3.1
Five Major Categories of Human Capabilities,
Representing the Outcomes of Learning with
Examples of Each

Learning Outcome	*Example of Human Performance Made Possible by the Capability*
Verbal Information	Stating the provisions of the First Amendment to the U.S. Constitution
Intellectual Skill	Showing how to do the following:
Discrimination	Distinguishing printed b's from d's
Concrete Concept	Identifying the spatial relation "below"
Defined Concept	Classifying a "city" by using a definition
Rule	Demonstrating that water changes state at 100° C.
Higher-Order Rule	Generating a rule for predicting rainfall, given conditions of location and terrain
Cognitive Strategy	Originating a novel plan for disposing of fallen leaves
Attitude	Choosing swimming as a preferred exercise
Motor Skill	Executing the performance of planing the edge of a board

the five categories is listed, along with an example of the
kind of performance from which the capability can be
inferred. The subcategories of intellectual skills are separately identified with examples, since the distinctions
among them and their ordered relationships are of importance for instruction.

By reference to the table, and having digested this chapter, the reader will probably be able to supply a number of additional examples of human performances corresponding to each category of learned capability. This exercise would be a valuable one. Whatever their basis in neural functioning, these categories of learning outcomes have differing implications concerning arrangement of conditions for their learning and retention, as we shall see in the next chapter. Thus, the planning and conduct of instruction must be carried out with full awareness of these differences, in order to be successful in achieving learning goals.

General References

Varieties of Learning Outcomes

Bloom, B. S., Hastings, J. T., & Madaus, G. F. *Handbook on formative and summative evaluation of student learning.* New York: McGraw-Hill, 1971.

Gagné, R. M., & Briggs, L. J. *Principles of instructional design.* New York: Holt, Rinehart & Winston, 1974.

Intellectual Skills

Gagné, R. M. *The conditions of learning.* (2nd ed.) New York: Holt, Rinehart & Winston, 1970.

Motor Skills

Fitts, P. M. & Posner, M. I. *Human performance.* Belmont, Calif.: Brooks/Cole, 1967.

Singer, R. N. *Psychomotor domain: Movement behavior.* Philadelphia: Lea & Febiger, 1972.

Attitudes

Fishbein, M. (Ed.) *Attitude theory and measurement.* New York: Wiley, 1967.

Mager, R. F. *Developing attitude toward learning.* Belmont, Calif.: Fearon, 1968.

Triandis, H. C. *Attitude and attitude change.* New York: Wiley, 1971.

Cognitive Strategies

Bruner, J. S. *Toward a theory of instruction*. Cambridge: Harvard University Press, 1966.

Bruner, J. S. *The relevance of education*. New York: Norton, 1971.

Chapter 4 Conditions for Learning

The process of learning has several distinguishable phases. Its purpose is the establishment of internal states or capabilities. The five major varieties of these learning outcomes were described in Chapter 3. The process of learning must be supported by events occurring both outside and inside the learner. Support for learning outcomes can be conceptualized in a general way—it must enhance motivation, direct attention, provide the means of coding and retrieval, promote retention and transfer, and furnish feedback to complete the learning act. Having described the different meanings of "What is learned," we must now address the question, "How can support be given to *each* kind of learning outcome?"

To answer this question, we must examine the specific events that facilitate learning for verbal information, for intellectual skills, for cognitive strategies, for attitudes, and for motor skills. We call these events the *conditions for learning*. Some of these conditions, to be sure, are essentially the same for all five kinds of learning outcomes. Others are quite dissimilar, and it is these to which we will give particular emphasis in this chapter. Learning conditions can form the basis of a theory of instruction, which in turn can guide the activities of teachers in planning and conducting instruction.

Before proceeding with our description of learning conditions, however, we must consider again the types of learning outcomes. This step follows logically from the discussion in the previous chapter, and it will also help to set the stage for further treatment of the events of instruction. From this point on, we want to be able to speak of the various capabilities to be learned as learning *objectives* —that is, verbal descriptions of what is to be learned.

Objectives for Learning

In our later discussion of the conditions for learning, we will refer to the objectives of the learning, sometimes called *instructional objectives*. (They are also sometimes called "behavioral objectives," a term not used here, but which we understand to mean simply the "objectives of learning as reflected in student behavior.") Naturally, learning objectives are related to learning outcomes; in fact, they are derived from them. To define and state an objective for learning is to express one of the categories (or subcategories) of learning outcomes in terms of human performance and to specify the situation in which it is to be observed.

Statements of Learning Objectives

Suppose, for example, that a proposed capability to be learned is verbal information, and that the subject-matter is the First Amendment to the U.S. Constitution (see the example in Table 3.1). The learning objective can readily be specified by describing the *situation* confronting the learner, the outcome *verb* denoting the class of capability learned (which in this case is "to state"), and the *action* which the learner is expected to take in order to exhibit this outcome. One can readily put together a complete description of the learning objective as follows:

(Situation): Given the question, "What are the provisions of the First Amendment to the U.S. Constitution?";
(Outcome performance): States the provisions (freedom of religion, speech, press, assembly, petition);
(Action): Writing.

In this statement, as in subsequent examples, the parts of an objective statement are identified in parentheses.

The description of the objective may of course be more or less detailed, depending on the purposes for which the statement is to be used. For an instructional designer or a teacher, this example probably contains about the right amount of detail. For purposes of designing a test of the performance, more specifics may be needed. If the objective is to be communicated to the student, a somewhat more informal statement like the following may be appropriate: "You should be able to tell us what the First Amendment prohibits." Thus, a learning objective need not have a precise content. Its expression varies according to the expected recipient of the communication it makes; and this may be different for a teacher, a test-maker, a parent, or a student. Sometimes, the *situation* and the *action* are understood and do not need to be stated; sometimes, additional description of *tools* or *means* are necessary. The essential core of the learning objective, however, must be included in every case: This is the *outcome verb* and its predicate. This verb identifies what is learned as one of the types of capabilities described in Chapter 3.

Although the uses of learning objectives will be referred to a number of times in this book, it may be desirable here to make note of the several purposes of communication they serve.

1. For the *teacher*, statements of learning objectives constitute a basis for the planning of instruction, for the conduct of teaching, and also for checking on the completion of learning.

2. For the *student*, appropriate communications of learning objectives may be an important element in the establishment of motivation and the feedback from completed learning.

3. For the school principal or educational *manager*, learning objectives provide a basis for the accountability of the educational program for which he is responsible.

4. For the *evaluator* of instruction, objectives serve to define the domains of performance which he will attempt to assess or measure.

5. For the *parent*, the communication of suitably phrased learning objectives serves the highly useful purpose of informing him about what his son or daughter has been learning (as opposed to what classes he has been attending).

Examples of Learning Objectives

Using the varieties of learned capabilities described in Chapter 3, the examples of Table 3.1 may readily be represented as *defined learning objectives*. The results of this transformation are given in Table 4.1. In each case, as will be seen, it is necessary to describe the *situation* considered appropriate for the observation of the performance; customarily, this description begins with the word "Given . . . ." The most essential part of the objective statement, the *outcome performance*, follows, beginning with an appropriate outcome *verb*. For this purpose, the verbs suggested previously in Table 3.1 serve admirably. The next element in the statement is the *action*, typically described by a gerundive form of a verb, as "by writing." It may be noted that this action word is *not* a highly important part of the objective statement (in contrast to the outcome verb); it merely indicates the particular form the performance is to take and is often chosen for convenience of observation.

Finally, for the sake of completeness, the objective statement may need to include the *means* or *tools* the learner will use, as in "on a scale from 1 to 10" (see Higher-Order Rule, Table 4.1).

Table 4.1
Examples of Learning (Instructional) Objectives for Categories of Learning Outcomes

Learning Outcome	*Objective*
Verbal Information	(Situation) Given the question, "What are the provisions of the First Amendment to the U.S. Constitution" (Outcome performance) *states* the provision (Action) by writing
Intellectual Skill Discrimination	(Situation) Given a sample printed "b" and rows of randomly sequenced "b's" and "d's" (Outcome performance) *distinguishes* the b's (action) by underlining them (Means) in pencil.
Concrete Concept	(Situation) Given several pictures containing familiar objects arranged one below the other and the oral direction "Mark the object *below* the (*familiar object*)" (Outcome performance) *identifies* the "below" object (Action) by marking (Means) with pencil.
Defined Concept	(Situation) Given an aerial photo of terrain including a city (Outcome performance) *classifies by definition* the city as a population and transportation center (Action) by describing and referencing these features on the photograph.
Rule	(Situation) Given the direction, "Show that water changes its state at 100° C" (Outcome performance) *demonstrates* the change from liquid to gas (Action) by heating the water, measuring its temperature, and observing its state (Means) using Bunsen burner, thermometer, and other appropriate tools

Table 4.1 (continued)

Learning Outcome	Objective
Higher-order Rule	(Situation) Given a terrain map of a section of the country and information about prevailing winds (Outcome performance) *generates* predicted relative rainfall in designated areas of the section (Action) by writing numerals (Means) on a scale from 1 to 10.
Cognitive Strategy	(Situation) Given the question, "How would you design an original method to dispose of fallen leaves without burning them?" (Outcome performance) *originates* one or more methods of disposal (Action) by writing descriptions of them.
Attitude	(Situation) Given descriptions of several situations in which facilities for physical exercise are available and the time appropriate (Outcome performance) *chooses* swimming over other alternatiaves (Action) by checking this choice (Means) on a scale indicating choice likelihood.
Motor Skill	(Situation) Given a board 1″ × 4″ × 20″ and the direction "Make one edge smooth and straight" (Outcome performance *executes* (Action) by planing the edge (Means) with a jack plane.

As previously noted, various kinds of rephrasing may be done without changing or making ambiguous the meaning of a learning objective. Various components of the statement may be omitted, or others added, to serve different uses. The core of the statement, without which an objective is useless, is the *verb for outcome performance.* The verb *states* means that the human capability being learned is verbal information; *demonstrates* means that a rule is being learned; *chooses* means that the learning expected is an attitude, and so on. Although these exact verbs may be replaced by others which convey the same meaning, the verb in the learning objective must be unambiguous, without question. The main idea to be communicated, after all, is what kind of human capability is to be learned?

Learning Conditions

In a sense, learning objectives provide a view of learning "from the back end forward." As we shall see, the main reason for this view is to keep firmly in mind what the "ends" of learning are. It is time now, however, to give further consideration to the means of approaching each of these ends and by so doing, adopt a forward-looking view. Assuming that one knows what the ends should be, how does one get there? This question must be answered in terms of the learning phases described in Chapter 2. In the sections devoted to each type of learning outcome that follow, we shall describe the external conditions that are distinctive for each, as they apply to the various phases of learning.

The reader may find it helpful to think of each type of capability, as we consider it, as a learning objective. The examples of Table 4.1 may serve as prototypes for those the reader wishes to generate for himself. In each case, the most important component to keep in mind is the outcome verb—the clue to "what is being learned."

Verbal Information

What distinctive external conditions need to be arranged to bring about the learning of verbal information? What should the teacher be concerned with, as a designer and deliverer of instruction, if the student is expected to acquire information?

Apprehending. Verbal information may be presented in several different ways which arouse attention and direct selective perception. When presented orally, variations in the loudness and intonation of speech are often employed, a fact well known to public speakers and lecturers. When the information is presented in printed form, attention may be directed to important features of the communication by the use of variations in type, color, indentations on a page, underlining, and other elements of design. Pictures or diagrams are sometimes employed primarily to arouse attention. In television presentations, rapidly shifting action sequences (as in *Sesame Street*) have proven effective in holding the attention of young viewers.

Acquisition. The process of coding that occurs during this learning phase is of critical significance for the learning of verbal information. In the most general sense, coding is enhanced when information is presented within an *associated meaningful context*. Several particular means are used to provide this meaningful context.

1. Advance "organizers." The work of Ausubel (1968) has shown the effectiveness of presenting items of information to be learned within contexts of "advance organizers." These consist of verbal material which is, on the one hand, a reminder of something the learner already knows and, on the other, an organization of information that is more general and inclusive than the specific information to be learned. Normally, the "organizer" is introduced before the new information which is to be acquired. In one of Ausubel's studies, for example (Ausubel and Fitzgerald, 1961), the learners' knowledge of the main principles of Christianity was employed as an organizer for learning the principles of Buddhism. The new information was "subsumed" into a larger framework of knowledge and, at the same time, differentiated from it. The general point of Ausubel's study is that individual facts and generalizations are more readily learned and retained when they are related to a more inclusive "framework" of meaningful knowledge, the latter being of the sort that is already available to the learner.

2. Meaningful coding of names and labels. Individual facts such as names and labels may be efficiently coded by placing them within larger structures such as sentences. For example, the work of Rohwer and Lynch (1966), cited in Chapter 2, showed that children learned word pairs such as LION-HORSE with considerably greater success when they were presented as sentences like "The LION scares the HORSE" than when they were presented in conjunctive phrases such as "The LION and the HORSE." Simple coding devices of this sort are often very useful to the human learner. For example, the name of a flower like the marigold might be conveniently coded by means of the sentence "MARY's petals turn to GOLD." Techniques of coding are examples of the kinds of cognitive strategies that may be acquired by the learner.

3. Imagery.   Another kind of meaningful context may be provided by an image, usually a visual image (Bower, 1971; Paivio, 1971; Crovitz, 1970). For example, a series of events may be coded in terms of a visual image of a room or a street; the properties of an object may be coded in terms of a spatial "map." Techniques of this sort have been used for many years by professional memory experts. Although these elaborate systems are perhaps of no general value for the learning of information, nevertheless, it may be acknowledged that the human memory naturally "works" this way and, therefore, that coding by imagery may be beneficially employed. Often, this can best be done by suggesting the form of the imagery to the learner, rather than by providing an actual picture or diagram.

Recall and generalization.   Both retrieval of information and its transfer to new situations are affected by external events which occur during the initial learning. The key point here is that recall is aided when the *cues* to retrieval are presented in association with the information to be learned (and remembered). For example, suppose the student will be asked to recall facts about the duties of a state governor at a later stage in a course when he is learning the duties of a city manager. Cues helpful to this act of recall can be given at the time the initial facts are presented. In this case, these cues would probably best be presented in a context of meaningful information, which briefly mentioned outstanding points of similarity and difference between the duties of governor and city manager.

Cues associated with originally learned information may also be expected to aid in the generalization of this information—that is, in its transfer to new situations of learning or use. Although the full range of future situations may be difficult to predict, transfer can be supported by providing a *variety* of contexts during initial learning. For example, the provisions of the Fourth Amendment pertaining to searches and seizures may be illustrated by concrete examples of house entry, arrest, phone-tapping, and so on. These varieties of examples become the sources of later transfer of the information to new situations and to additional learning.

Intellectual Skills

External events influence the processes underlying the learning of intellectual skills in ways that differ from those events most relevant to the learning of information, as the following paragraphs indicate.

Acquisition.   Learning a new intellectual skill is essentially a matter of "snapping into place" a combination of simpler skills that have previously been learned. For example, suppose that the learner is expected to acquire the skill represented by problems such as this: "$a - 2b = 14; a = 20$; what is the value of b?" This skill is composed of several simpler skills, including (1) substituting numerical values for variables in an equation; (2) "transposing" terms; (3) subtracting two-digit numbers; and (4) dividing by small numbers. If the learner has acquired these simpler component skills, acquisition of the new skill is primarily a matter of "putting them together" in the proper order. When the conditions for learning are properly arranged, the event of acquisition occurs with a suddenness that is often accompanied by a feeling of pleasant surprise on the part of the learner.

When subordinate skills are combined to form a new and more complex skill, they must occur in a suitable sequence. In the example given, the transposing of terms must be done before the subtracting of two-digit numbers, and the latter in turn must be done before the dividing operation is carried out. Thus, the "combination" that constitutes the newly learned skill usually involves learning an *ordering* of the simpler skills of which it is composed.

Any intellectual skill may be analyzed into the simpler skills which must be combined to bring about its learning. By such analyses, it usually becomes evident that the simpler skills which represent the "immediate prerequisites" can themselves be analyzed to reveal the even simpler skills of which they are composed (Gagné, 1970, pp. 237-276). This process of analysis reveals what is called a *learning hierarchy*, which is nothing more or less than a chart of the subordinate skills related to some particular complex skill that is to be learned. An example of a learning hierarchy related to a science topic is given in Figure 4.1.

Two major kinds of external events influence the acquisition of intellectual skills. First, the simple skills that are to be combined must be *retrieved* to the working memory (that is, short-term memory). Sometimes this is done by a communication to the learner which says, simply, "You remember how to transpose the terms of an equation." On other occasions, it may be necessary for the performances representing the subordinate skills to be reinstated by having the learner show that he can actually do them.

A second kind of external event is the provision of *cues to sequence*, so that the combination of skills attains the proper order. The kind of communication used for this purpose often takes the form of a verbal statement like the following: "First you will need to substitute a numerical value for a; then you can transpose the terms; and now you can find the value of b." The extent to which such external cuing is necessary varies with the complexity of

Figure 4.1
A learning hierarchy indicating component skills in solving a problem in physical work.

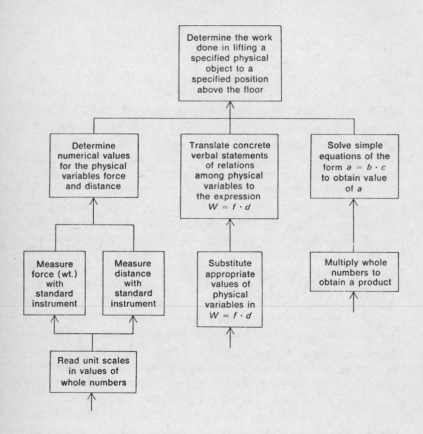

From Gagné, R. M. *The Conditions of Learning*, 2nd ed., copyright Holt, Rinehart and Winston, Inc., 1970. Reprinted by permission of Holt, Rinehart and Winston, Inc.

the skill to be learned and also with the learner, that is,

with the extent to which he is able to provide the cues himself. Sometimes, cuing of this sort may be reduced to a "hint," or even omitted altogether. When cues are omitted, the method is called "discovery learning" (Shulman and Keislar, 1966).

Recall. Although intellectual skills such as rules and concepts may be rapidly learned, the process of retrieval sometimes presents difficulties. When the learner searches his memory for cues to the ordering of the skill or for specific information associated with it, he may find the skill inaccessible. His feeling is—I know *how* to do this, but I have forgotten *what* it is. Retrieval of fully learned intellectual skills may turn out to be relatively poor, even a few days following their learning. An example is provided by the rule for converting readings of Fahrenheit temperature to the Celsius scale. The learner may have acquired this skill and yet suffer forgetting, in the sense that he cannot retrieve the set of cues which will enable him to reinstate it. Various cues may be provided externally to "jog his memory," such as "5/9," or "—32," or the formula $C = 5/9(F - 32)$. Thus, it is sometimes necessary for the learner to retrieve verbal information as a cue for the retrieval of the intellectual skill.

Another way external events may be used to influence the retrieval of intellectual skills is by the conduct of *reviews*, typically *spaced* over days or weeks of time. When the learner is asked to recall an intellectual skill, for example, by being asked to solve a problem involving that skill, he uses his processes of retrieval to obtain access to the skill in his memory. In so doing, he is using his own cues to search and recover the skill. In other words, he is practicing retrieval, and such practice has been shown to be effective in insuring the retention of intellectual skills (cf. Reynolds and Glaser, 1966).

Generalizing. Intellectual skills are important components in the transfer of learning. It is common to distinguish two kinds of transfer in which such skills are involved. In *vertical transfer*, intellectual skills exhibit transfer to "higher-level" skills, that is, to skills which are more complex (Gagné, 1970). The intellectual skill of multiplying whole numbers, for example, is a part of the more complex skills of dividing, adding, and multiplying fractions, finding square roots, solving proportions, and many others. Transfer to the learning of these more complex skills is dependent primarily on the *prior learning* of the simpler skills. The more basic skills must be "mastered," in the sense that they can be readily retrieved, in order for transfer to take place to the learning of the more complex intellectual skills. This principle is illustrated by the learning hierarchy, an example of which is shown in Figure 4.1.

The second kind of transfer is called *lateral transfer*. This refers to the generalization of what is learned to new situations, differing from those in which learning has occurred. Skills are transferred in this sense when they are used in pursuit of some new intellectual activity. The transfer of rules and concepts to new situations and problems is a process which is also subject to the influence of external events in the learner's environment. The process itself bears some resemblance to retrieval, except that it requires the use of additional cues to relate it to the new situation. Accordingly, there is evidently some advantage to having the learner practice the application of the skill to a *variety* of situations or problem contexts. For example, if the learner has acquired the skill of reading decimal values from a scale by interpolation, transfer is enhanced by asking the learner to retrieve the skill in reading many different kinds of scales—foot rules, meter sticks, pressure gauges, thermometers, and others.

Cognitive Strategies

In considering the third major type of learning outcome, we find a different set of external influences that can be brought to bear upon the processes of learning. Since cognitive strategies are internally organized control processes, the effects of external conditions on their learning is found to be less direct than is the case with verbal information and intellectual skills.

Acquisition. The strategies that govern the individual's own behavior in attending, learning, remembering, and thinking are not learned on single occasions, which is the case with intellectual skills. Instead, they undergo refinement over long periods of time. It is this characteristic that makes them appear to be described more appropriately as *developed* rather than *learned*. The extent to which inherent growth of the central nervous system determines the rate of such development has not been determined. The theory of Piaget (Flavell, 1963) proposes that there are stages of growth that set limits to cognitive strategy development at a range of age levels: the sensorimotor period (zero-two years) the preoperational period (two-seven years) the period of concrete operations (seven-eleven years) and the period of formal operations (eleven years to adult).

Irrespective of such limits, if indeed they do exist, it is apparent that learning plays an important role in the development of cognitive strategies. Some of the simpler strategies, which are applicable, for example, to attending and coding, can apparently be established by direct instruction and practice. Rohwer (1974) has reviewed a number of studies concerned with the use of "elaboration strategies" in the learning of associations of word-pairs (such as DOG-GATE, GIRL-CHAIR). Presumably, such strategies create shared meanings between the words of the pair, when these words are related to each other either by being presented in sentences ("the DOG ran through the GATE") or shown in pictures. Young children (ages six-eleven) learn and remember word-pairs most readily when these sentences or pictures are explicitly shown. Older learners, however, sometimes acquire and recall the word-pairs more readily when they are told to supply the sentences or the mental pictures themselves. Such results imply that the older learners have available effective coding strategies to call upon and use, whereas the younger children do not. Other studies (Levin, Davidson, Wolff, and Citron, 1973) have shown that children as young as age seven can learn to use strategies of sentence and imagery elaboration in learning to identify pairs of objects (presented as words or pictures).

Procedures for teaching cognitive strategies of problem solving have usually combined the presentation of verbal descriptions of the strategy with practice in solving a variety of problems. Such a method is used, for example, in the *Productive Thinking Program* (Covington, Crutchfield, Davies, and Olton, 1972). The approach and results of this program have been described by Olton and Crutchfield (1969). Children are given a set of booklets providing "guided practice" in problem solving. Each booklet describes a detective-type mystery problem for the child to solve. As the story unfolds, printed verbal instructions describe certain strategies to the student, introduced one at a time. Examples of the strategies included are: (1) how to generate many ideas; (2) how to evaluate the relevance of ideas to facts; (3) how to look at a problem in new ways; (4) how to ask relevant questions; (5) how to become sensitive to useful clues; (6) how to clarify the essentials of the problem. The student practices such skills in connection with each problem, and writes down his ideas, questions, or suggestions for what should be done next. Results of studies using this method have shown substantial improvements in the problem-solving performances of fourth and fifth grade children, when tested on a set of entirely new problems of varied content.

Direct verbal description of useful cognitive strategies may be an effective way of arranging suitable conditions for learning them, at least in many circumstances. Following such instructions, however, the learner needs to be given opportunities to employ the strategies and perhaps refine them, by meeting a variety of problem-solving situations. Providing *frequent opportunities for the practice* of cognitive strategies is most important. For example, if one wishes to promote the development of good strategies of problem solving in students, the best method presently known is to challenge them on frequent occasions to solve novel problems. In this way the individual learns to select, organize, and utilize the strategies available to him that govern his own thinking processes.

Feedback.   The feedback phase of the learning process has a particularly cogent function to perform in the learning of cognitive strategies. The reinforcing events provided to the learner must be *informative* about what has actually been accomplished. The principle here is simple in conception: If the learner has been challenged to be original, or invent-ive in his execution of a performance involving a cognitive strategy, the feedback should indicate the nature and amount of originality, creativeness, or inventiveness. Thus, the setting of a problem situation, or successive problem situations, is no more than half the battle, so far as arrang-ing suitable learning conditions is concerned. The other half, equally important, is the condition of feedback, in which the learner has his originality (or whatever) con-firmed.

Attitudes

As we have seen in Chapter 3, an attitude is a learned capability that affects the learner's choice of personal action. Thus, an attitude is an internal state that originates processes of *executive control* (Figure 1.2).

Attitudes may be learned in a "direct" manner, or in ways that are "indirect." When directly acquired, they may result from the experience of success on the part of the learner. Receiving reinforcement for successful per-formance in an amateur theatrical effort, the learner is likely to acquire a positive attitude toward acting as a personal activity. If the student has experienced success in painting, his attitude toward painting will tend to make him choose it as a leisure-time pursuit. By generalization, his attitude toward viewing the work of other painters may also be affected. On a simpler level, the student's liking for the study of any school subject is affected by the reinforcement he receives from successful achievement in that subject (Mager, 1968).

The principal indirect method of establishing and modifying attitudes is by human modeling (Bandura, 1969). In this method, the acquisition phase of learning should be preceded by measures to insure that the learner respects or "identifies with" the human model, who may be a teacher, parent, or a well-known popular hero. After a model has been selected, the steps in instruction for attitude are approximately as follows:

1. The learner observes the human model making the desirable choice of personal action. For example, the teacher may be observed helping a child; a prominent sports figure may be observed rejecting the offer of a harmful drug.

2. The human model is observed to take pleasure from his action or to achieve success in it. For example, the baseball player may be seen to maintain his alertness and vigor and thus to make a successful double play.

3. By observing such demonstrations, the learner is reinforced "vicariously" (Bandura, 1971). This increases the likelihood that he will make choices of personal action similar to those made by the human model he has seen.

As this description implies, the processes involved in the modification of attitudes may be strongly influenced by external events in the learner's environment. Again, the critical features of these events are quite distinctive in relation to those applicable to other kinds of learning objectives.

Motivation.   The establishment of an expectancy is a particularly critical feature in the learning of an attitude. If the learner has experienced success following a choice of personal action, a reminder may be sufficient to activate the expectancy. For example, if the individual has chosen to attend a concert of classical music and has participated in the enjoyment and public appreciation of the performance, a reminder of this success may activate the expectancy which is the first step in acquiring a positive attitude towards such action. When a human model is a part of the motivating situation, as opposed to personal experience of the learner, the model must be an admired or respected person, one with whom the learner "identifies." In this case, the expectancy is presumably one of "becoming like" the admired person.

Performance. Executing the performance resulting from the choice of action is an essential part of learning an attitude. For example, if the attitude to be learned is one of liking to read modern fiction, the reading of several such works (with suitable feedback confirming an expectancy of enjoyment) is of particular importance to the learning. When human modeling is employed, the choice of action is displayed to the learner; the choice is made by the model, rather than by the learner himself. In such instances, the model's behavior in making such a choice needs to be shown or described. For example, a person acting as a model may be shown to evidence concern for the feelings of another, when such an attitude is the desired objective for learning.

Feedback. As our previous discussion has already implied, reinforcement during the feedback phase of learning is of critical importance in the establishment or modification of an attitude. The expectancy which is activated during the motivational phase must be confirmed in order to complete the act of learning. Success following the choice of personal action may be directly experienced by the learner, as when he chooses golf as an activity and finds he can drive the ball onto the green most of the time. When the choice of action is observed in a human model, the confirmation takes the form of "vicarious reinforcement" (Bandura, 1971). The learner must observe the model being rewarded, or attaining the satisfaction of his (the model's) goal, following the choice of action he has made. Thus, in the case of a model rejecting an offer of harmful drugs, the consequences of this action, such as winning a race in the high hurdles, need to be displayed to the learner.

Motor Skills

We come now to the fifth and final major type of learning outcome, the motor skill. Here again, external events have a particularly critical influence on the internal processes of learning.

Acquisition. Two different components of the motor skill must be taken into account. First, there is the learning of an *executive subroutine* (Fitts and Posner, 1967), which governs the number and sequence of actions that make up the performance. This is actually a rule for procedure. In learning to print the letter E, for example, the child must learn to make four distinct strokes and adopt a particular order for these strokes. The learning of this procedure may be facilitated by certain kinds of verbal communications, such as "first make a line downward, then three lines across."

Besides the rule-governed procedure, the accuracy and smoothness of performance constitutes the essential component of the learned motor skill. Since such skills are influenced by feedback from muscular movement, their control by external sources of stimulation must be indirect. This is usually accomplished by *practice*, that is, repeated attempts on the part of the learner to achieve the desired performance. In the case of printing E's, the child may spend considerable time printing E's which progressively approach the shape of a printed model.

Performance. Practice, of course, involves performance on repeated occasions. This is an obvious point, restated here only to emphasize again that the occasions on which external stimulation is presented need to be followed by the involvement of muscular action and by the consequence of some "product," such as a printed E or the passage of a basketball through the hoop.

Feedback. As in the case of other learning outcomes, the expectancy which initiated the learning of the skill needs to be confirmed. There is some evidence to indicate that the *immediacy* of reinforcement may be important in facilitating the learning of motor skills. It is not always easy to arrange feedback for motor skills without some delay. For example, typing students are not usually aware of having made an error in striking a letter until they check over a page containing many lines of their work. This situation contrasts with that of a skill like throwing darts, where the accuracy of the throw is almost immediately made apparent by the position of the dart on the board. Generally speaking, the evidence shows that feedback given immediately following the performance is an aid to learning (Merrill, 1971).

Besides immediacy, the *informative accuracy* of feedback has been found to exert a facilitative influence on the learning of motor skills (Fitts and Posner, 1967, pp. 27-33). Thus, in general, learning processes are more likely to be supported when the learner is told how close he comes to a target performance, as opposed to being told simply that he is "doing well." The child's learning of printing letters is aided by the provision of standards with which he can compare the products of his own performance.

Learning Conditions in Instruction

The processes of learning, remembering, and transfer that take place within the learner can be influenced by external events in the learner's environment. Each phase of learning, as described in Chapter 2, is potentially subject to the influence of externally generated stimulation. The degree to which such influence may be applied, however, and the extent of the influence, depends upon *what is being learned*. Accordingly, we found it necessary in Chapter 3 to distinguish the five major classes of learning outcomes—verbal information, intellectual skills, cognitive strategies, attitudes, and motor skills. These five kinds of learning outcomes may be expressed in statements of *learning objectives*. In this chapter, we have described for each outcome (or objective) the external events that appear to be involved critically in the support of its learning.

The activity of planning and executing external events to support learning processes aimed at particular types of objectives is called *instruction*. The various modes of instruction will be considered in later chapters. At this point, it can be realized that the very conception of instruction is made possible by these potentialities for the external influence of learning processes. Table 4.2 summarizes the critical external conditions for learning we have mentioned in this chapter.

Using Learning Conditions in Instruction

The items in the second column of Table 4.2, which have been described more fully in the preceding section, state *what is being accomplished* by the external conditions of learning. Various means are used by the designer of instruction and by the teacher to bring about these results. It may be desirable, as a forerunner of what is to come in later chapters, to attempt to draw some generalizations from the information shown in Table 4.2. Some of the ways in which external events are used to influence learning occur again and again. What are some of the *general* things that are done in instruction?

Stimulating recall.   Sometimes, the external events accomplish their purposes by stimulating the learner to recall (and retrieve) something he had previously learned. This may be done by giving a simple reminder ("Remember that you know how to subtract two-digit numbers"); or by

Table 4.2
A Summary of External Conditions Which Can
Critically Influence the Processes of Learning

Class of Learning Objective	*Critical Learning Conditions*
Verbal Information	1. Activating attention by variations in print or speech 2. Presenting a meaningful context (including imagery) for effective coding
Intellectual Skill	1. Stimulating the retrieval of previously learned component skills 2. Presenting verbal cues to the ordering of the combination of component skills 3. Scheduling occasions for spaced reviews 4. Using a variety of contexts to promote transfer
Cognitive Strategy	1. Verbal description of strategy 2. Providing a frequent variety of occasions for the exercise of strategies, by posing novel problems to be solved
Attitude	1. Reminding learner of success experiences following choice of particular action; alternatively, insuring identification with an admired "human model" 2. Performing the chosen action; or observing its performance by the human model 3. Giving feedback for successful performance; or observing feedback in the human model
Motor Skill	1. Presenting verbal or other guidance to cue the learning of the executive subroutine 2. Arranging repeated practice 3. Furnishing feedback with immediacy and accuracy

asking the learner to reinstate something he has learned ("First, show me the nouns in this sentence"). Stimulating recall is of particular importance in the case of intellectual skills, when component skills need to be remembered. It is also of value in reminding the learner of previous "successes" when an attitude is being established. Recall may be necessary for any particular instance of learning, regardless of the class of learning outcome.

Direct presentation of stimulation. Naturally, the environmental stimulation inherently involved in the learning task must be directly presented to the learner. If he is asked to read a French sentence, he must have the printed sentence before him; if he is expected to identify musical intervals, he must hear the tones. Beyond these obvious instances, however, are other examples of using direct stimulation to influence learning processes. Varied stimuli (underlining, colored printing) may be employed to arouse attention. Pictures, tables, or diagrams may be presented to suggest ways of coding the information to be learned. Verbal or pictorial cues may be given to support the retrieval of what has been learned.

Activation of a mental set. A third means of influencing learning processes is by the activation of a *mental set*. A set is usually induced by verbal instructions. It selectively activates processes of learning and performance. Thus, if the learner is directed to "attend only to the shapes of this group of figures, not to their colors," the set so established will control the process of attention when the figures are shown. If the directions are "learn and remember only the 'animal' words in the list that will be read to you," the resulting set will activate the learner's coding and retrieval processes in such a way that the "animal" words are learned and remembered. Of course, the learner may give himself instructions that establish one or more sets, and thus activate his own processes—in fact, this commonly happens when the learner undertakes to learn "by himself."

Providing feedback. Every act of learning requires feedback if it is to be completed. Sometimes feedback is automatically provided by the performance itself, as when a ring is tossed over a pole. In many instances, however, provision must be made to communicate the outcomes of a learned performance as accurately as possible. The degree to which a learner-printed E conforms to a standard, the completeness of the learner's information about a historical event, the adequacy of his comprehension of a reading passage, and the originality of his solution of a novel problem are all examples.

It may be realized, then, that the teacher has at his disposal at least four general ways of influencing learning processes—by stimulating recall, by direct presentation of stimuli, by activating mental sets, and by providing feedback. These are the four most general components of *instruction*, and they are used to bring about the critical learning conditions summarized in Table 1.3. Additional examples of their use are discussed in the following chapters.

General References

Learning Objectives

Mager, R. F. *Preparing objectives for instruction*. Belmont, Calif.: Fearon, 1962.

Popham, W. J., & Baker, E. L. *Systematic instruction*. Englewood Cliffs, N.J.: Prentice-Hall, 1970.

Conditions for Learning

Ausubel, D. P. *Educational psychology: A cognitive view*. New York: Holt, Rinehart & Winston, 1968.

Bandura, A. *Principles of behavior modification*. New York: Holt, Rinehart & Winston, 1969.

Gagné, R. M. *The conditions of learning*. (2nd ed.) New York: Holt, Rinehart & Winston, 1970.

Learning and Instruction

Bruner, J. S. *The relevance of education*. New York: Norton, 1971.

Gagné, R. M., & Briggs, L. J. *Principles of instructional design*. New York: Holt, Rinehart & Winston, 1974.

Merrill, M. D. *Instructional design: Readings*. Englewood Cliffs, N.J.: Prentice-Hall, 1971.

Chapter 5 Planning Instruction

A teacher has many things to do, and one of his most important activities is making sure that the learning of students is supported in every possible way. The previous chapters have described the nature of learning processes and learning outcomes and, thus, have indicated the *potential* ways in which student learning can be influenced. In this chapter and the next, we propose to discuss how procedures of *instruction* can be devised and used to make these potential influences become actualities.

Two Aspects of Instruction

Like many complex human activities, instruction has two parts to its accomplishment. Because it is complex and subject to the various constraints of specific situations, it must first be *planned*. Teachers may plan specific "next assignments" for particular students. They may plan lessons for groups or classes of children. They frequently plan a set of topics to be included as part of a year or semester course and often the course as a whole. Sometimes, too, they plan larger programs or "curricula," either independently or as members of a team. Again as team members, they may be called upon to plan an educational program for an entire school or school system, such as a program of independent study or of environmental education.

The second component, following the planning, is the conduct of instructional "operations" or the *delivery* of instruction. Here the teacher may be arranging an external supporting situation for an individual student, a small face-to-face group, or a larger group like a class. Teachers may be engaged in motivating, stimulating recall, or in any of the other kinds of learning-support activities implied by Chapter 4. They may be communicating to students verbally, demonstrating how to do something, displaying some phenomenon before a class, or behaving as human models in adjudicating disputes. Thus, besides the planning the teacher has done in preparation for instruction, many moment-to-moment decisions are required for instructional delivery.

The planning of instruction will be dealt with in this chapter, leaving the matter of delivery to the next. It will be desirable to describe first the basis for planning large units of instruction like courses and topics and then proceed to the individual lesson and its component events. In connection with individual lesson planning, we shall need to pay particular attention to those instructional events which are of critical relevance to the different kinds of learning outcomes described in Chapter 4. Throughout these descriptions, we continue to have in mind the question, "How can instruction be planned to support the processes of learning most effectively?"

The Planning of Courses

Instructional planning is frequently done in terms of relatively large units such as *courses*. Naturally, such a unit of instruction may occupy various periods of time, from a few days to many months, and a definition of "course" in terms of such time intervals is not a matter of concern here. A course is often conceived as containing several *topics*, each of which in turn may have a number of different instructional objectives. Thus, a course in American government might include topics on local government, state government, the Congress, the court system, and so on. Each topic in its turn may be further subdivided into subtopics and then into lessons.

Teachers sometimes plan entire courses, although the structure of such courses may often be provided by a textbook or other curricular materials. Within such frameworks, many kinds of adaptations can be made to insure the best usage of the course materials. In some cases, teachers or teams of teachers may undertake to plan a series of topics or an entire course. Here we shall describe course planning without regard to the question of whether the materials are being designed initially or whether they are selected from existing texts and adapted for classroom use.

The rules of planning applicable to courses and topics are primarily the rules of outlining, in which the more inclusive entities are broken down into logically subordinate ones. In addition, a course whose content contains a time frame, like history, may be organized in sequences corresponding to the natural progression of the events it includes. These organizational principles are logically based and have no particular concern with the goal of promoting learning, except insofar as a logically sensible organization may help to establish a favorable student attitude. In contrast to topical outlining, the defining of specific objectives, as described in the previous chapter, is most appropriately done within a topic or within a lesson. There are, however, two aspects of course planning that may have an influence on learning—the identification of *multiple learning goals* and the arrangement of *sequences of prerequisites*.

Multiple Learning Goals

The course and topic, and even the subtopic, are seldom designed to achieve a single type of learning outcome. Typically, the course or topic is expected to attain two or more of the kinds of learning goals described in Chapter 3—verbal information, intellectual skills, cognitive strategies, attitudes, and motor skills. A course in public speaking, for example, is usually designed to bring about not only the learning of rules for precise oral communication (*intellectual skills*), but also the acquisition of an *attitude* of "projecting to an audience" and probably the *cognitive strategies* involved in originating an extemporaneous speech. A course in American Government typically has multiple goals: the acquisition of *information* about the forms and procedures of government, an *attitude* of respect for democratic processes, and probably also *cognitive strategies* applicable to the solution of social problems.

It is of some importance to adequate course or topic planning, therefore, to identify various types of learning objectives and to make suitable provision for each of them. The course designer may begin his planning with multiple objectives in mind, but the details of planning may "carry him away" so that he neglects something he really intended to include. For example, a teacher wishes to design a topic with the outcomes of (1) information about harmful drugs and (2) an attitude unfavorable to the abuse of drugs. As planning proceeds, a great deal of information is collected about drugs, their composition, common names, and effects upon the human body. This information can be skillfully organized and put in a meaningful context, perhaps including tables and diagrams. When the plan is finished, it may be admired as an excellent example of a well-organized presentation. But what has become of the *attitude* as a goal? The designer will readily see that almost no provision has been made for this goal. Thus, if the topic is to fulfill both of its purposes, it must be redesigned.

Procedures of instructional planning to insure the identification and inclusion of multiple outcomes may be aided by two kinds of "editing." First, one can check to see that certain important features of instruction relevant to the proposed learning outcomes have been included. (These are the critical learning conditions suggested by Table 4.2.) Second, by applying an "outcome question," one can insure that the instruction being designed is indeed likely to reach its intended objective. Cues to both of these editing procedures are displayed in Table 5.1.

As shown in Table 5.1, the designer of a course or topic that is intended to establish the capability of *verbal information* might ask himself two editing questions as he proceeds with the design: (1) Has a meaningful context been provided, and are there suggested ways of coding the information to be learned and stored? (2) When the topic has been completed, will the student be able to state the desired information (orally or in writing)? Similar questions pertaining to instructional features and outcomes are listed for the other types of capabilities to be learned. Their systematic application to course and topic planning should help to maintain the goals of multiple outcomes.

Prerequisite Sequences

Quite apart from the logical or time-ordered sequences of instruction units inherent in the content of a course or topic, there are sometimes reasons for *sequencing* relating to the support of learning. Intellectual skills typically require the prior learning of simpler component skills (for example, see Figure 4.1). The sequences of skill learning thus implied will be described more fully in the next section, dealing with planning the individual lesson. Sometimes, however, prerequisite skills may overlap several topics of a course. For example, the identification of the factors of a number may initially be learned in the arithmetic topic, multiplication, but it also occurs in the topics of division and fractions. Similarly, in English instruction, the agreement of verbs and pronoun subjects may initially be learned in a topic on pronouns, but is encountered again in the topics of sentence and paragraph writing.

Table 5.1
Features of Instructional Planning for Courses and Topics, for Five Types of Expected Outcomes

Type of Expected Outcome	Instructional Features	Outcome Question
Verbal Information	Meaningful context; suggested coding schemes, including tables and diagrams	Will the student be able to *state* the desired information?
Intellectual Skill	Prior learning and recall of prerequisite skills	Will the student be able to *demonstrate* the application of the skill?
Cognitive Strategy	Occasions for novel problem solving	Will the student be able to *originate* new problems and their solutions?
Attitude	Experience of success following the choice of a personal action; or observation of these events in a human model	Will the student *choose* the intended personal action?
Motor Skill	Learning of executive routine; practice with informative feedback	Will the student be able to *execute* the motor performance?

Other kinds of learned capabilities may also have desirable prerequisites, although their relationships may be somewhat less direct than is the case with intellectual skills. The learning of information, when coded as organized knowledge, requires that the learner know the meaning of the words or phrases that make up the information; that is, he must know them as *concepts* (a type of intellectual skill). The learning of attitudes often implies prerequisite information or intellectual skills. For example, if the desired outcome of a lesson is an attitude tending toward avoidance of harmful drugs, the student must have acquired (usually in a prior lesson or topic) information about situations in which harmful drugs are likely to be encountered, their common names and appearances, and other items of this general sort. Should such information not be provided as a prerequisite, the intended choice of action for the student would not be clear to him and, therefore, would likely not be made.

Some of the most readily identifiable prerequisites for the five major types of learning outcomes are listed in Table 5.2. They are stated in general terms and are intended to guide the process of course and topic planning. Not all the possible prerequisite relationships are covered by the contents of the table, however, since many different variations may be found to depend on specific circumstances. The procedure suggested is again of the "editing" sort: The course designer continues to question himself as to whether the learning of any particular kind of intended learning outcome must be preceded by the learning of a prerequisite capability.

Table 5.2 indicates that when *verbal information* is to be coded and stored as organized knowledge, steps must be taken to insure that the meanings of the words are known; in other words, that the concepts referred to have been learned. The sentence "Mice harbor parasites," for example, can be coded and stored as knowledge by learners who have previously acquired the concepts "harbor" and "parasite," assuming that "mice" is already known. Of course, the meanings of these words may be acquired during a single lesson, or they may have been introduced during an earlier topic.

Table 5.2
Possible Prerequisite Relationships
in the Design of Courses and Topics

Type of Expected Outcome	Possible Prerequisite Learning
Verbal Information (Knowledge)	Referent meanings of words, i.e., concepts
Intellectual Skill	Component simpler skills Information specific to the application examples
Cognitive Strategy	Intellectual skills involved in problem solution Information involved in problem solution Masses of organized knowledge
Attitude	Prior success experience following choice of desired personal action Identification with human model Information and skills involved in the personal action
Motor skill	Executive routine controlling performance Part-skills or motor chains

The learning of an *intellectual skill* requires prior learning of simpler component skills. In addition, the application of the skill to particular examples may require prior knowledge of certain information. For instance, the application of the intellectual skill of "solving a proportion" might be contained in a problem such as the following: "What force is required to bring a lever into equilibrium about a fulcrum when the force on one end is twenty grams, three meters from the fulcrum; and the force to be found is applied at the other end, five meters from the fulcrum?" Obviously, applying the appropriate rule for proportion in this instance will demand that the learner have prior information relating concepts such as "lever" "fulcrum" and "equilibrium" to each other. Such information is likely to have been introduced by plan in a previous topic.

When novel problems are used for the learning and improvement of *cognitive strategies* of thinking, they too may demand the use of previously acquired intellectual skills and verbal information. The designer of a course will surely wish to avoid the circumstance in which a student is "challenged" to find a solution to a problem which he is unable to solve simply because he does not possess essential information or skills. Not only should problems be chosen carefully to avoid this situation, but provision must be made for a sequence of topics in a course that will provide the information and skills needed for solving problems.

Still another function of previously learned information can be identified as a factor in the development of cognitive strategies. Research studies have often shown that originality of thought is related to amount of organized knowledge (Johnson, 1972). Most truly original thinkers are people who have vast stores of knowledge in many fields. Thus, the acquiring of information, whether in previous topics of a course or even in other courses, is likely to have relevance to the development of productive thinking strategies.

Attitude modification usually depends upon the experience of success following a choice of personal action. Such success may be planned to occur, or at least the opportunity provided for it to occur, in earlier parts of a course or in an earlier period of time. A positive attitude toward "helping others" for example, may be initially introduced in a small way, by encouraging a child to find a chair for a classmate. This incident (presumably pleasant) may then be used at a later time as a basis for more elaborate "helping" behavior choices, such as aiding in a search for lost mittens. When the approach of human modeling is used, the prerequisite requirement is that the learner respect or otherwise identify with the "model." Again in the case of attitudes, information and intellectual skills may be prerequisites; that is, the behavior aimed for must be within the student's repertoire, as established by prior learning.

In learning a *motor skill*, the executive subroutine that

controls the sequence of responses may have been previously learned. In learning to turn an automobile around on a two-lane road, for example, the executive procedure of forward turning left—backward turning right—forward turning left, and so on must be kept constantly in mind by the novice driver, as he continues to practice the motor skill of controlling the car's movement by means of the accelerator pedal and steering wheel. Still another kind of learning which may be planned for an earlier stage of a course is the learning of part-skills. In swimming instruction, for example, the part-skill involving leg movements is often practiced separately from the total skill of the crawl, before being put together with other part-skills.

Thus, the planning of sequences of instructional components that compose a course or topic frequently requires attention to *prerequisites*. The course planner is concerned with the question of whether each new lesson or topic has been preceded by the learning of capabilities that adequately prepare the learner to undertake the new learning expected of him. Since new learning is often a matter of "combining" capabilities that can be made accessible in memory, course planning must insure that these capabilities have been previously learned.

Planning the Lesson

Once topics and subtopics have been identified and placed in a suitable sequence, instructional planning can proceed to concern itself with the individual unit of instruction, which we shall call the lesson. As conceived here, the lesson has no fixed time characteristics, nor can the scope of its coverage be specified exactly. In the typical classroom setting, the lesson is often planned to require the time of a class period, say, forty-five-fifty minutes. However, a lesson may also be designed as a student project, which is expected to be accomplished in several hours spread over a longer period of time—days or weeks. Or, a lesson may be a single laboratory "exercise" to be undertaken by a pair of students or a small group and to extend over several class periods. In general, whatever its duration, a lesson has a *single primary goal* as its expected outcome. That is to say, the typical lesson may be identified as having a primary learning objective that falls into one of the classes of verbal information, intellectual skill, cognitive strategy, attitude, or motor skill.

It should be noted, however, that although a primary goal identifies a lesson, there is usually more than one secondary goal as well. For example, when an intellectual skill like "writing a unified paragraph" is the primary goal, the same lesson may also give some attention to an attitude such as "preferring to read self-produced paragraphs which have unity." In addition, such a lesson may well be concerned with the practice of cognitive strategies when it includes an assignment such as "Write an original paragraph describing the effects of a sudden, unexpected event such as a loud clap of thunder." Practical instruction seldom attains the purity of a single learning event or a single type of learning outcome.

The Events of a Lesson

Planning a lesson is mainly a matter of taking care to insure that each process described in Chapter 2 has been supported in an optimal fashion by external events. One must keep in mind the expected outcome for learning (see Table 5.1) and the special conditions each requires. In a more particular sense, however, attention must be paid to the series of *external events* that can influence the various learning processes, as they were described in Chapter 4. The events to be described in the following paragraphs follow that outline of learning processes. The events of the lesson occur roughly in the order described here, although this order is not considered an inviolable one.

1. Activating motivation. The internal conditions of learning involved in the motivational phase arise in part from long-lasting expectancies which are stored in the learner's memory. These are often referred to simply as *motives*. There are many kinds of motives—fundamental wants like the need for food; social motives such as desire for social approval, prestige, and affection; personal motives like curiosity and the desire for power or dominance. It is not possible to deal with varieties of motives in this book or do little more than acknowledge their existence. The desire for mastery or *effectance*, as pointed out in Chapter 2, appears to be one of the most dependable motives on which to base the design of instruction. However, many different motives may play a part in learning on any particular occasion. Discovering what they are and setting them into motion is an important task for the teacher to undertake in lesson planning.

The initial events of a lesson are often designed to re-arouse motivational states in the learner. The introduction to a lesson often does this by "appealing to the interest of the student." A science lesson on the use of the microscope may be introduced in terms of the "detection of clues." This approach would appeal to the student's curiosity, and to his desire for social approval originating in his knowledge that the detective is a person admired for his skill. Or, a lesson in English literature may be introduced by a communication which explains that the principal character in the short story to be read is trying to work out a personal psychological problem—thus appealing to the desire of the student to develop a "good personality." Obviously, there are many ways to arouse interest and many prevailing motives to call upon. The effective teacher usually becomes quite skillful in devising ways to make instruction "relevant" to student interests.

2. Informing the learner of the objective. The second component of motivating events is the establishment of a relatively specific *expectancy* concerning the outcome of learning. Often, this more specific outcome must be related to the general motivational state, as when the student is led to see that knowing how to identify microorganisms with a microscope will enable him to detect water impuri-

Figure 5.1
Activating student motivation.

A few years from now, you will be buying gasoline for your car by the _liter_. Your model airplane will use smaller fractions of a _liter_.

This container holds a _liter_ of liquid—about a quart. But how can we know how much to ask for if we only want a small amount?

Model airplane

ties. But beyond this, a specific expectancy of the learning outcome of the lesson needs to be established. This is usually done by means of a _set_ (see p. 94) which persists throughout the act of learning. The set may be established when the teacher, or the textbook, communicates to the learner _what he will be able to do when learning has been completed_. Using the example of the microscope again, the student may be told that when learning is completed, he will be able to identify several specified types of microorganisms in pond water. If the lesson is in arithmetic, the communication to the student may establish a set that he will (when learning is complete) be able to divide a fraction by a fraction; if in language, the student may come to realize that he will be able to choose the use of *who* and *whom.*

3. Directing attention. Often, the next event in the lesson is directing attention to the stimuli which are an inherent part of the learning task. In many instances, attention may be directed by simple communications such as "Look at this series of numbers," or "Notice the subject and the verb in this sentence." Of course, this commonly used method assumes that students have already acquired habits of responding to such communications. Young children may not have acquired such habits and therefore will need to learn them as instruction proceeds, using the methods of "behavior modification" (Homme, Csanyi, Gonzales, & Rechs, 1970; see also the volume by Baer in this series).

More precise methods of directing attention may also be employed, particularly when selective perception of certain features of the external stimulation is required. When the sounds of letters are being learned by children, for example, greater intensity may be given to sounding of specific letters within syllables, as in "A, rA, rAt"—when the sound of the vowel a is to be learned. If the growing parts of a plant are to be identified as an objective of a science lesson, these parts may be separately outlined and labeled in a diagram to which the student refers while making his observations. In the learning of a geometric rule such as "Triangles are similar when two of the angles of each are equal," the angles of two triangles may be outlined heavily in a diagram so that attention is drawn to them.

4. Stimulating recall. One additional kind of event is often required as a part of instruction, before the new learning actually takes place. As we emphasized earlier in this chapter, various previously learned capabilities (prerequisites) need to be made readily accessible in the fore-

Figure 5.2
Directing attention.

front of the learner's memory. Different means may be employed in instruction to stimulate recall and recovery of these previously learned entities. One can simply say "Remember that you learned how to interpolate values between those shown on a scale"; or "Remember what 'freezing' means." Communications of this type often accomplish the purpose of making prerequisite learnings accessible from the student's memory.

Sometimes, however, the recall of necessary capabilities may require more than a simple reminder—for instance, when the prior learning has occurred a fairly long time ago or when there has been inadequate opportunity for intervening review. In such instances, a more elaborate event, in

Figure 5.3
Stimulating recall of prior learning.

which students actively *reinstate* what has previously been learned, may need to be arranged. Thus, before proceeding with a lesson whose objective is "making personal pronouns agree with verbs," the teacher may first set the task: "Write a list of all the personal pronouns." This list would then be checked over by the students, with feedback from the teacher, to insure that all had fully recalled the pronouns and thus were ready to proceed with the new learning. Or, if the lesson had the objective of "classifying types of urban transportation," the teacher might find it desirable to have the students recall the definition of a city. The students might be asked to "Write an outline to show

how the definition of a city applies to _____ (a city shown in an aerial photograph)." Again, this exercise would have the purpose of insuring the accessibility of previously learned capabilities.

5. *Providing learning guidance.*   At this point in time, the acquisition phase of learning is ready to occur, including the encoding of what is to be learned and its entry into memory storage. Generally speaking, the events that form a part of instruction during this learning phase may be called *learning guidance.* These events are differentiated in their emphasis, in accordance with the particular kind of learning objective that is intended, as indicated in Table 4.2. Thus, if the learning of verbal information is the intended outcome, the accompanying learning guidance takes the form of a meaningful context; if a rule is to be learned, guidance may be provided by a verbal statement cuing the sequence in which subordinate rules are to be combined; and so on.

The amount of learning guidance provided, that is, the length and complexity of the communication or other form of stimulation, varies with a number of factors in the situation. For example, to a group of bright students applying newly learned arithmetic rules to verbally stated examples, the teacher may find it desirable to provide a minimal amount of guidance, or none at all, and thus to emphasize "discovery learning." For somewhat less able students, guidance might take the form of "hints" or "prompts," which carefully avoid "giving the answer away." Turning to a different kind of learning, motor skills, it is evident that learning guidance may concern itself with the cuing of the executive subroutine, as in "taking the proper stance." Beyond this, however, verbal guidance is known to be of little use for motor skills; the learner must practice the motor act.

Perhaps the most general common characteristic to be sought in learning guidance is its orientation to the objective. In whatever form it is given, whether as verbal state-

Figure 5.4
Providing learning guidance.

ments, "hints," diagrams, or pictures, its purpose is to insure a form of *encoding* which will enable the learner later to recover what he had learned and display it as some kind of performance. It is essential that examples of situations are included, which will later be encountered by the student and which become sources of cues to retrieval. Thus, the verbal communication, set of cues, or diagram chosen to provide learning guidance is not to be selected because of its logical or esthetic qualities, but rather because it helps the *learner to store and recall* what is being learned. In designing this aspect of the lesson, the teacher will find it useful to keep firmly in mind the outcome to be expected, that is, what the student will be able to do when learning is completed.

6. Enhancing retention. Instructional provisions for enhancing retention and retrieval of what has been learned take the form of *spaced reviews.* Spacing means requiring recall at reasonable intervals, of a day or more, following the initial learning. It is customary, for instance, to provide a number of examples calling for application of a newly learned capability immediately after learning is completed. Requiring more than two or three review examples is relatively ineffective, however, so long as the examples are to be done immediately. The recall of the learned capability is greatly enhanced when additional examples are spaced in time over days or weeks following the initial learning.

Figure 5.5
Enhancing retention by an additional example.

It is desirable for spaced reviews to include a variety of situations. For example, if the student has initially learned to form ratios in connection with areas, the examples employed in spaced reviews might be designed to require application to ratios of distance/time, and voltage/resistance, and weight/volume. If the student has learned to define "legislative" in terms of the national Congress, examples in spaced reviews might require application of the definition to state legislatures and city councils. Variety in examples is known to enhance retention, presumably because it enables the student to acquire additional internal cues which he can use to search his memory.

7. Promoting transfer of learning. In making use of learning transfer to promote new learning within a course or subject (transfer in the *vertical* sense), it is essential to provide for the prior learning of prerequisite information and intellectual skills. For this reason, a lesson may include questions or problems which have the double purpose of: (1) probing for the presence of these prerequisite capabilities, and (2) making sure they are currently available in the student's "working memory." Such activities may not always occupy much time, but they are of critical importance in making use of the advantage learning transfer gives to the acquisition of new capabilities.

When transfer of learning to other fields of study or activity (*lateral* transfer) is aimed for, support is provided by a variety of examples and situations. In large part, transfer of the lateral sort appears to depend upon the effectiveness of memory search and retrieval carried out by the learner when he confronts new situations to which his previously learned capabilities must be applied. Accordingly, the promotion of transfer is brought about by instruction which provides novel tasks for the student, spaced over time, and calling for the use of what has previously been learned. Often, these novel tasks take the form of problem-solving situations—undertaking a project, composing an essay, solving a mathematical puzzle, designing an investigation of a natural phenomenon.

Figure 5.6
Promoting transfer of learning.

8. *Eliciting the performance; providing feedback*. The occasion on which the performance that represents the learning outcome is elicited may, of course, take place as an initial event preceding a series of spaced reviews or transfer tasks. Usually, this event is conceived as a kind of terminal action to the event of learning itself. Regardless of how simple the performance may appear (particularly when one also has in mind transfer to novel situations), it is important to provide an occasion for the display of the performance by the student. Having learned, the student needs to "show what he can do," not only for the teacher's purposes, but for his own learning. The display of the performance needs to be closely coupled with *informative feedback*, in order for reinforcement to occur. If the student has learned to locate a position on the globe in terms of latitude and longitude, for example, the performance

Figure 5.7
Eliciting the performance; giving feedback.

might be elicited by asking him to find the position of the city of St. Louis. When latitude and longitude are reported by the student, he is then given feedback as to whether these are correct or to what extent and in what way they differ from the correct values.

Relating Instructional Events to Learning Processes

Each external event of instruction is designed to influence one or more of the internal processes of learning. A pictorial representation of these relationships is given in Figure 5.8. In this figure, the phases of learning and their underlying processes (from Figure 2.1) are shown opposite the events of instruction appropriate to each phase. The figure provides a summary of instructional events, as described in the preceding paragraphs of this section, and indicates their timing as related to learning phases.

Figure 5.8
Relation of the phases of learning to instructional events.

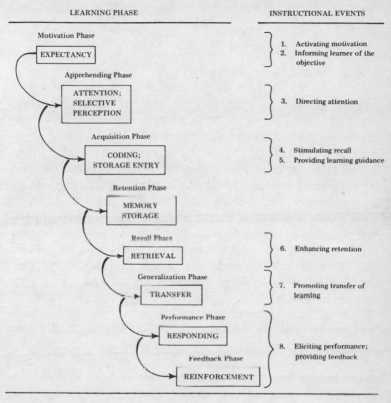

LEARNING PHASE	INSTRUCTIONAL EVENTS
Motivation Phase EXPECTANCY	1. Activating motivation 2. Informing learner of the objective
Apprehending Phase ATTENTION; SELECTIVE PERCEPTION	3. Directing attention
Acquisition Phase CODING; STORAGE ENTRY	4. Stimulating recall 5. Providing learning guidance
Retention Phase MEMORY STORAGE	
Recall Phase RETRIEVAL	6. Enhancing retention
Generalization Phase TRANSFER	7. Promoting transfer of learning
Performance Phase RESPONDING	8. Eliciting performance; providing feedback
Feedback Phase REINFORCEMENT	

Self-Instruction and Learning

As we have emphasized throughout this book, the instructional events designed to be carried out during an act of learning (several of which may occur during a single lesson) have the purpose of stimulating, activating, supporting, and facilitating the internal processes of learning. Any of these events may be useful in achieving these purposes for any specific lesson or lesson component, or all of them may be. However, it should be clear that the particular events which need to be planned for any given learner, or for any group of learners, cannot be predicted with precision. Individual differences among students are large, at all ages, and must be taken fully into account in the planning of instruction.

Differences in Self-Instruction

The student differences of particular relevance to the planning of instruction are those pertaining to the *amount of self-instruction* the students are able to undertake. Obviously, a skilled adult, such as a college senior or university graduate student, arranges virtually all the events of instruction for himself. For him, learning is typically a matter of reading a book or several books. If he is a truly sophisticated learner, he is already motivated. He sets his own objectives, adopts an attentional set, uses an efficient coding system, devises novel ways of applying what he has learned, demonstrates to himself the performance of which he is capable, and verifies the product so as to provide feedback. In other words, he brings to bear on his own learning a whole set of *procedural rules* and *cognitive strategies* that eliminate the necessity for most kinds of "external" instruction.

Most learners, however, are not as skilled as the true "self-learner." Instead, they are still acquiring the procedures of learning (sometimes called "study habits") and the cognitive strategies which activate and guide their own learning processes. The external events of instruction are designed: (1) to provide the support needed in activating learning processes, and (2) to encourage the development of the cognitive strategies which will make such external support unnecessary. As an ultimate goal, it may be said that instruction should be designed to "put itself out of business." But that is not an easy goal to attain, and it surely cannot be done over short periods of time. According to experience as currently appraised, developing a student into a truly independent learner takes years. This is the basic reason why organized programs of instruction exist—to fill these years with learning.

Choosing Instructional Events

The instructional events the teacher chooses to omit from the total set listed in Figure 5.8 should be those which, as an estimate, are not required because the students can supply them themselves. First-graders, in general, would not be expected to be capable of managing their own learning processes. Sixth-graders may be able to assume sets to direct attention and to use moderately effective strategies of coding and retrieval. High school students should be able to instruct themselves in many of the capabilities they are expected to learn. But these are generalities only. The teacher must decide, for each specific learning act, which instructional events might be omitted and which need to be emphasized.

The following list is intended as a guide for estimates of the potentiality for self-instruction and, therefore, for the planning of instructional events:

1. *Activating motivation* can be omitted as an event when the motivation of learners is obviously high or when the lesson ties in with known student motivations. For much of instruction, though, it is an event of high importance.

2. *Informing the learner of the objective* of a lesson is almost always a good idea, except when the objective is already apparent.

3. *Directing attention* can often be done very simply. Sometimes, special pains must be taken to emphasize features for selective perception.

4. *Stimulating recall* may not be necessary for skillful self-learners; for others, however, it may be a critical event.

5. *Providing learning guidance.* This event may also be omitted when skill in self-instruction can be relied on.

6. *Enhancing retention.* Provisions for this event need not be made for highly skillful learners. Others, not so skillful, may need to be reminded to practice retrieval.

7. *Promoting transfer* is almost always a useful event, since it confronts the learner with novel situations that he may be unable to devise by himself.

8. *Eliciting performance, coupled with feedback* can be

omitted for only the most skillful self-learners. It is this event which completes the learning, and to omit it would be a serious mistake.

Obviously, including more instruction than is necessary is likely to lead to boredom on the part of students. Providing less than is needed, however, has the serious consequences of inadequate learning, misdirected learning, or no learning at all. Making good estimates of student self-instructional capabilities is an essential part of the planning of instruction.

General References

Learning and Instruction

Merrill, M. D. *Instructional design: Readings.* Englewood Cliffs, N. J.: Prentice-Hall, 1971.

Instructional Planning

Briggs, L. J. *Handbook of procedures for the design of instruction.* Pittsburgh: American Institutes for Research, 1970.

Gagné, R. M., & Briggs, L. J. *Principles of instructional design.* New York: Holt, Rinehart & Winston, 1974.

Popham, W. J. & Baker, E. L. *Planning an instructional sequence.* Englewood Cliffs, N. J.: Prentice-Hall, 1970.

Tyler, R. W. *Basic principles of curriculum and instruction.* Chicago: University of Chicago Press, 1949.

Chapter 6 Delivering Instruction

Once instruction has been planned, it must be delivered to students. The teacher can choose many ways to deliver instruction, and these may be combined to form a variety of patterns of external stimulation to the learner. The teacher's voice in delivering meaningful communications is a common mode, as is the printed presentation of sentences in a pamphlet or textbook. In addition, there are actual objects such as clocks, blocks, beads, rabbits; models like those of cities and buildings; pictures and diagrams; pictures showing motion via television or film; and a variety of sound-producing devices. Any and all of these sources of stimulation may be woven into a great variety of combinations to perform the instructional functions discussed in Chapter 5.

The selection, orchestration, and delivery of stimulation

by means of these various sources comprise a large portion of the decisions the teacher must make every day. Sometimes, the selection made is a critical one; for example, in learning to understand spoken French, the student must be presented with oral samples of French, and a printed representation of such speech will not suffice. On other occasions, the decision is not so critical; for example, a suitably prepared student may learn a new fact equally well by hearing it spoken or by reading it in a text. The ultimate guide to decisions about the sources of instructional stimulation is the learning objective.

276, Another important area of decision making for the teacher is the matching of instructional events to the *numbers* of students they are intended to influence. There are striking individual differences among students and consequent differences in the effectiveness of various kinds of external stimulation. Assuming that the teacher is responsible for the instruction of twenty-five to forty students, there are many ways of arranging these students for purposes of delivering instruction. They can, of course, be treated as a total group; they can be arranged in several smaller groups; or they can work in twos or threes, as is common in doing science exercises. Moreover, a certain portion of student instruction, which may be more or less extensive, is delivered to the *individual*.

In this chapter we shall attempt to describe the bases for teacher decisions about ways of delivering instruction, keeping in mind the available sources of stimulation, but with emphasis on the different ways of arranging groups of students, or individual students, to receive and profit from instruction. Thus, we shall need to consider how the events of instruction can best be delivered, and what the limitations on their delivery are, for groups of class size, for smaller interacting groups within the class settings, and for the individual student.

Instruction in the Class

Modern school classrooms are typically quite flexible in

permitting various arrangements of students into large and small groups, and allowing even for individual work by students outside any group. The days of fixed seating of students in classrooms are long gone, and the availability of movable furniture, modular units, screens, and other equipment of this nature make possible many kinds of student groupings.

Although the frequency of "class" instruction has undoubtedly diminished, there are still many occasions in the school on which this size of student group is given instruction. What kinds of instruction can be most effectively conducted with groups of class size? How can the necessary instructional events be delivered to such groups? What limitations does this size of student group impose on instructional effectiveness?

Instructional Events in the Class Setting

Perhaps the most obvious characteristic of any class is that it is composed of individuals. The differences in performance, and in capability of performance, that these individuals display are large. There are differences in learning outcomes among individuals that can scarcely be lessened, regardless of how effective instruction may be in attaining commonly shared goals. Sometimes less obvious, although of no less importance, are the individual differences in the capabilities that different learners *bring to* a common learning task—differences in their "entering capabilities." These entering capabilities constitute the raw material with which instruction must work.

How can instruction in a class setting deal with individual differences in what students bring to the learning activity? Are there advantages, and also limitations, to be expected of instruction in the class setting? These questions may be considered in terms of each of the events of instruction described in Chapter 5.

Initial instructional events. In the conduct of initial events of instruction, the teacher's task includes the activities of activating motivation, informing students of objectives, and directing attention to relevant aspects of lesson materials. In all these instances, the decisions being made by the teacher are based on estimates of such items as *what will appeal* to all the members of the class and what will hold their attention. These tasks may be readily accomplished for classes of students whose family backgrounds are relatively homogeneous. Obviously, they demand great ingenuity when students exhibit a wide range of backgrounds. Of course, if the teacher were acting as a tutor for a single individual, these estimates could be made more exact. In any case, they require that the teacher be well acquainted with members of the class as individuals.

Stimulating recall; providing learning guidance. These instructional events make great demands on a teacher's skill. They are often difficult to accomplish efficiently, because of the individual differences in entering capabilities of students. Suppose, for example, the lesson objective is "using the objective case of pronouns which are objects of prepositions" (for *her*, about *him*, between *us*, etc.). The teacher may begin by asking students to recall one or more important prerequisites, for example, what a preposition is, what pronouns are in the objective case, and so on. The difficulty lies in insuring that all members of the class have in fact retrieved these capabilities from their memories. By the time the next learning event occurs, a few will not have done so; many will; and some may become inattentive because it takes so long for the recall performance of other students to occur.

The next event, guiding the learning, is also complicated by the fact of individual differences. If the teacher uses the method of "discovery learning," he might present several examples ("He sits next to *her*; she stands between *them*, etc.") and ask that the rule be stated. How many students would be able to do this? The likelihood is that a fair proportion would not. Alternatively, the teacher might proceed with this event by communicating the rule "When pronouns are objects of prepositions, they are used in the objective case." Hearing this, how many students would then be able to complete sentences like the following, using pronouns correctly: "It is strictly a matter between me and——"? Perhaps a majority would, but possibly all would not.

Various means are used to overcome these difficulties of class instruction. Small groups of students may be formed whose members have mastered a common set of prerequisites, and for whom the estimates of needed recall and effective guidance can be more precisely estimated. Different small groups may proceed to attain the same lesson objectives by spending more time recalling prerequisite skills and perhaps by receiving more detailed learning guidance, such as more hints, fuller prompts. Another widely employed method is to arrange instruction so that initial learning (of a new rule, for example) is done individually by students. Programmed instructional material may be used for this purpose. More frequently, students undertake individual self-instruction by studying a text for homework. A third method, also frequently used, consists in the teacher's calling for responses from members of the class who "need it most." In following such a procedure, the teacher uses his knowledge of individual students to estimate which ones are most likely to need to reinstate previously learned capabilities in order to "recover" them; and which students are most likely to need "hints" or other kinds of cues to encoding.

Enhancing retention and transfer.   Individual differences among class members again present the teacher of the class with problems in pursuing the aims of enhancing retention and promoting transfer of learning. Some students in a class may have acquired strategies of retrieval that are highly effective; others may not. Suggestions of retrieval techniques and cues (such as tables, diagrams, pictures, or verbal "hooks"), having been chosen to be most effective "on the average," are typically given to the entire class.

Their effectiveness, however, is bound to vary, owing to the idiosyncratic nature of individual memory stores. Alternatively, the teacher may urge students to "use their own schemes" for retrieval. For those students who already have efficient schemes (cognitive strategies) for retrieval, this method should work very well. For those who do not, individual suggestions may be valuable.

Spaced reviews of previously learned capabilities provide opportunities for processes of retrieval to be set in operation and thus constitute an important method of enhancing retention. Such reviews may be, and frequently are, conducted with an entire class. Again, in this situation, the teacher usually makes decisions about "who most needs to be called upon," when asking for responses from individual class members. Under such circumstances, some students will receive direct practice in retrieval; others may practice "to themselves" in anticipation of being called upon; and still others may not retrieve at all. An alternative method for review is a quiz, or test, in which all students face the necessity of retrieving by writing answers to a common set of questions.

Problem—solving tasks are often employed to promote transfer of learned capabilities to novel situations. Choosing suitable tasks requires an estimate that the component intellectual skills and information involved in problem solving are available to all members of the class. To the extent that they are unavailable to any students, both the problem-solving process and its outcome will be degraded in quality and scope. For example, a problem for a class in social studies might be one of predicting the growth of stores in a local shopping center, based upon the projected pattern of housing in the surrounding area. Reasonably original solutions to such a problem require a number of skills on the part of the students—the construction of graphs, extrapolation of trends, and the concepts of ease of transportation, population density, family income, and others. Students who have indeed attained these intellectual skills will be able to participate in the process of solving the problem in ways that are valuable for their learning. Students who have not attained these skills will, in a class situation, simply be acquiring some not very useful information by listening to other students.

The conduct of *class discussions*, another variety of problem-solving situation, is often plagued by these same difficulties. Ideally, the class discusssion is an excellent way to promote transfer of learning. When members of a discussion group have available to them a common set of information and skills, they are able to display their originality of thought in a setting which provides valuable feedback from other members of the group. In such situations, reinforcement is provided for originality of thought, critical judgment, and facility in communicating ideas. Ideally, discussion is a most valuable method of instruction for a group of students. The ideal, however, is not achieved very frequently. In fact, the most frequent occurrence in discussion groups is the interjection of questions or comments which clearly indicate the absence of prerequisite knowledge and skills on the part of individual members.

Eliciting performance and providing feedback. Arranging these events for the class requires considerable ingenuity. A common method is for the teacher to call upon individual students. When such a procedure is used in the informal setting of the modern classroom, care should be taken to include those who do not volunteer as well as those who do; otherwise, an entire class period may be dominated by those students who learn most readily, to the detriment of others. In a class setting, it is not clear that at the time student A is responding students B through Z are profiting much from this instructional event. Some may be; and the feedback provided by a good performance of the reciting student may constitute reinforcement for these other students. But many of the students who are not answering will not be attending to the answer given by their classmates. For them, the performance and its feedback will not be having its best effect.

To overcome this difficulty, teachers often turn to the written test or quiz, which requires each member of the class to respond to a common set of questions. When such tests do not depend on speed of reading or responding, they constitute a perfectly good method of eliciting student performance. But how shall feedback be given promptly? Here again, a reasonably good method can be applied in most instances—the exchange of test papers and the marking of correct and incorrect answers by fellow students.

On occasion, student performance must be elicited in forms that are longer and more elaborate than a "quiz." This is particularly true when problem-solving tasks are assigned; as when students are asked to compare and contrast two forms of local government or to compose an essay on injustice. The essay test is used for this purpose, as is the paper or project assigned as homework. Naturally, tests and assignments of this sort imply a genuine commitment on the part of the teacher to read and comment on these products or at least to assign grades to them. It is just as important in using these procedures that the feedback be as prompt and accurate as possible.

Adapting Instructional Events to the Class

As this review of instructional events shows, the teacher makes a variety of decisions in adapting instructional events to the class setting. Individual differences among members of the class generate problems in selecting the means of influencing the learning processes of each student. Particular attention is required by those differences in the repertory of capabilities that students bring to the learning situation, and these, in turn, result mainly from prior learning.

Initial events of instruction in the class, such as the establishment of motivation and attention, can often be readily accomplished in a common way for all members of the class. For example, the introduction to a lesson on anthropoid apes, using pictures or movies, is likely to arouse the interest and attention of an entire class. Subsequent events, including stimulating recall, guiding the learning, providing for retention and transfer, and eliciting the performance and furnishing feedback, are more likely to require some differentiation for various class members. The teacher must choose among various techniques in order to influence the learning of individual students. In order to deal directly with each member, the teacher may spend some time tutoring individuals or divide the class into smaller groups. Often, a common learning task is assigned for each member of the class to work on independently, in the classroom or in homework. In addition, individual assignments such as papers or projects are made to each member of a class or to small teams. It is evident that the teacher has available several ways of "individualizing" instruction, and that these may be employed singly or in combination.

Instruction for the Individual Student

Two particular modes of instruction, emphasizing an orientation toward the individual learner, deserve separate discussion. First is the method which provides for interaction between two persons, the *tutorial* relationship. Second is the situation in which instruction is self-administered, often called *independent learning* (or *independent study*). As indicated in the previous section, both of these modes are employed with some frequency by the classroom teacher. Other instructional settings, however, may be designed to depend *primarily* on tutoring or independent learning. It will therefore be worthwhile to examine the nature of instructional events for each of these additional modes, and to compare them with the events of class (or group) instruction.

The comparison of instructional events for three modes of instruction is made in Table 6.1. The column labeled Group Instruction repeats in brief summary form the treatment of instructional events we have described for the class or group.

Table 6.1
Comparison of Instructional Events for Three Modes of Instruction:
Group, Tutorial, and Individual Learning

Instructional Event	Group Instruction	Tutorial Instruction	Individual Learning
Activating Motivation	Teacher establishes common motivation	Tutor discovers individual motivation	Student supplies own motivation
Informing Learner of Objective	Teacher communicates objective to group	Tutor communicates objective to student	Student confirms or selects objective
Directing Attention	Teacher stimulates attention of group members	Tutor adapts stimulation to student attention	Student adopts attentional set
Stimulating Recall	Teacher asks for recall by group members	Tutor checks recall of essential items	Student retrieves essential items
Guiding Learning	Teacher provides hints or prompts to group	Tutor provides guidance only when needed	Student supplies own strategies
Enhancing Retention	Teacher provides retrieval cues to group	Tutor encourages student to use his own cues for retrieval	Student supplies own retrieval cues
Promoting Transfer	Teacher sets transfer tasks for all members	Tutor sets transfer tasks adapted to student capabilities	Student thinks out generalizations
Eliciting Performance	Teacher uses a test to assess performances of group members	Tutor asks for performance when student is ready	Student verifies his own performance
Providing Feedback	Teacher provides feedback to students, varying in immediacy and precision	Tutor provides accurate and immediate feedback	Student provides own feedback

Tutorial Instruction

Comparisons of instructional events commonly employed in tutoring and in group instruction can be made by glancing down the center columns of Table 6.1. The tutor initiates the same kinds of instructional events as does the teacher of a group. Each event is, however, adapted to the particular needs and current learning status of the student. For example, the tutor is able to ask for recall of previously learned capabilities, which must be recovered by the particular student. He provides learning guidance only when the student obviously requires it. He suggests that the student use whatever cues he wishes for retrieval. He asks the student to perform when he is ready, and he is able to provide immediate feedback of considerable accuracy.

A valuable extension of the teacher's operation as a tutor is provided by student tutors. High school students may volunteer to tutor students in lower grades; junior high students may tutor pupils in elementary grades; fourth-graders may tutor first-graders. In nongraded classrooms, it is not uncommon to find tutoring of students by their peers. Students who have recently learned new information or intellectual skills often make excellent tutors for their classmates who have not yet learned the same items. In fact, many different combinations of tutors and students have been, and are continuing to be tried.

Student tutoring is frequently successful in accomplishing instruction, in improving achievement of tutors as well as their students, and in bringing about favorable changes in attitudes toward school learning (cf. Ellson *et al.*, 1965; Ellson, Harris, & Barber, 1968). Programs of student tutoring apparently work best when lessons have been carefully preplanned and when the tutors have been trained to administer the instructional events described in Table 6.1 (Niedermeyer & Ellis, 1970). The needed training, however, can usually be accomplished in a few days' time. Programs of student tutoring require careful management by teachers, particularly with respect to the selection and training of tutors, the preplanning of lessons, and the monitoring of student progress. Such programs are capable of yielding substantial benefits in the promotion of school learning (Gartner, Kohler, & Riessman, 1971).

Self-Instruction

The contrast of individual learning, or self-instruction, with other modes can be seen by comparing appropriate columns of Table 6.1. As an individual learner, the student begins a learning task with preestablished motivation. The teacher may have had a good deal to do with establishing such motivation, or it may have been established long ago. The student finds and confirms to himself the objective of the lesson in the textbook he is using or in the material he is studying. Alternatively, he may need to decide upon his own objective. For example, if he is studying a lesson in botany, he may decide that the objective is, "Show how nutrients from the soil reach the leaves of the plant." Such an objective may be selected by the student even though the textbook, film, or other medium does not state it explicitly.

Proceeding with the lesson, the self-instructing student adopts an attentional set which will best allow him to reach the objective he has in mind. That is to say, he reads, listens, and looks selectively for the communications he needs. If he needs to recall the concept "capillary action," he reminds himself of the meaning of this concept. Further, he uses whatever strategies are at his command to encode the capability being learned, so that retrieval will be possible and easy. He may, for example, think to himself, "I should remember the transport of nutrients through the stem to the leaf by means of a mental picture." If he is skilled in strategies for learning transfer, he may then establish some broader generalizations of what he has learned—whether there are differences and similarities in the transport of nutrients in large and small plants, in marine and land plants, and so on. In this way he may discover relationships that are entirely novel to him and not contained in the material he is reading or viewing.

The self-instructing student "knows" when he has achieved the lesson's objective. To make certain, he may set a problem for himself or rehearse his answers to questions about what he has learned. By carrying out these activities, the student is able to confirm the expectancy with which he began the learning task. Thus he is arranging for "self-reinforcement," and a feeling of satisfaction that he has in fact accomplished what he set out to do.

Individual learning obviously requires a great deal of the learner. To supply all the self-instructional sets and prompts that support learning in its various phases, the learner needs to acquire a number of cognitive strategies. A young child will have learned few of these strategies and will need much help from instruction by the teacher. As he gains experience, the student will be able to provide more and more self-instruction. By the time high school is reached, the "good" student will probably be able to do much learning on his own. When group classes are desirable, as in group problem solving and discussion, he will enter such groups prepared with the necessary skills and knowledge. But the student who is "less good" is the one who particularly needs the external support provided by instruction. Some phases of the learning process may go smoothly for him, but others will not. It is part of the teacher's job to find out which phases of learning are most likely to require external support and activation and which phases can be self-managed. In this way teaching can be adapted to subject matter, to age level, and ideally to the individual student.

Organizing Instruction to Include a Variety of Modes

School instruction normally includes all three modes of instruction we have described: (1) group (2) tutorial, and (3) individual self-instruction. The organization of instruction into these modes varies from grade to grade. In the primary grades, there is a good deal of tutoring of individual children, but there are also many occasions for small group instruction and activities for the total class group. In the intermediate grades, tutoring by the teacher is usually done less frequently, but sometimes occurs with students who have specific difficulties. In the junior high school, there is increasing emphasis on self-instruction in the form of project and homework assignments. The trend is continued into the high school, where many new learning tasks are originally tackled by the student on a self-instructional basis. This is the case, for example, when students study a new homework assignment in their textbooks, when they write a composition, or when they undertake an individual-study project.

In junior high and high school classes, instruction is often concerned with the support of the *recall* and *generalization* phases of learning. For example, suppose that students have studied (by self-instruction) a lesson on "the use of the definite article" in German. The next day's class is typically concerned with promoting retrieval of these rules by having students supply the definite article in new examples of German sentences. Transfer of learning may also be supported by conversation exercises which provide additional varieties of context for sentences using the definite article in different genders and cases.

A somewhat similar organization of instruction is to be seen in a social studies lesson on "checks and balances in federal government." Over a period of time, a class may have studied the powers of the legislative, executive, and judicial branches of government. This study has also been divided between the self-instruction occurring in homework and the recall exercises in following class sessions. Now there comes a time of "putting things together." This may be done by means of a class discussion, led by the teacher, in which novel questions are posed and commented on by members of the class. For instance, the teacher might pose the following question: "Suppose Congress were to enact a bill to prohibit the publication of comic books; what kinds of 'checks' would there be on such legislation?" To be successful, such a discussion requires that relevant prior knowledge has been learned.

Most probably, it has been acquired largely through self-instruction in homework assignments. The purpose of the discussion itself, however, is to enhance transfer of learning by engaging students in a group problem-solving situation.

Clearly, then, many kinds of instructional organization are available to classroom teachers. Varying degrees of emphasis can be placed upon the three modes of (1) group instruction, (2) tutoring, and (3) self-instruction, depending on the needs of particular circumstances. Generally, it is not desirable for teachers to attempt to force instruction into one mode at the expense of another—all three are useful. Age differences, subject-matter differences, and individual student differences must all be taken into account in organizing instruction. For the skillful teacher, decisions about instructional organization should come to depend heavily upon the answers to two questions:

1. What *kind* of capability is to be learned?
2. What *phase* or *phases* of instruction are to be undertaken in the time period for which planning is being done?

Making instructional decisions which are soundly based on answers to these questions should be possible for readers who have studied learning in this book. Teachers can, first, classify the objectives of instruction in the *categories* of information, intellectual skill, cognitive strategy, attitude, motor skill, or combinations of these. Next, it will be possible to see how these objectives are to be attained by learning—by the *processes* of expectancy through reinforcement which must occur for learning to be accomplished. Any given interval of student activity—a class period, a project, a homework assignment—can then be seen as containing *instructional events* designed to support one or more of these learning processes. At this point realistic decisions about organizing instruction become possible. For a particular student, or for a class of students, can these events best be made to happen by group instruction, by tutoring, or by self-instruction? Chances are a mixture will be chosen. The best mixture is one which is systematically organized, rather than put together at random; it is one which takes advantage of the strong features of each instructional mode. .

Using Audio and Visual Media

Our introductory comments to this chapter included the idea that the delivery of instruction often involves decisions about *media*. Besides the common media for instruction (the teacher's oral delivery, the blackboard, the textbook), there are some media that are more specialized in their uses and tend also to be based on more complex hardware. *Pictures* are more or less readily available to the teacher. Some are incorporated in textbooks, others are separately obtainable or capable of being constructed. They occur also in the form of slides and filmstrips. *Pictures with motion* are seen as films and in television programs. *Audio* presentations usually accompany the visual in motion pictures and television and appear by themselves in tape players, including the useful cassette players. *Combinations* of media (print, pictures, audio messages) may be put together in various ways by various devices. For example, slide-tape and filmstrip-sound combinations are frequently used in instruction. Surely the most elaborate media combination is provided by the use of the *computer* to manage and deliver instruction.

Audio and visual media are often particularly useful to the teacher in adapting instruction to the individual needs of students. For example, in the early grades, pictures are often employed to convey meaning to children who have not yet learned to read and also to provide concrete examples of concepts and rules that are being learned. Pictures, films, and television programs can serve a similar purpose for older students or adults who have difficulty in reading. Audio presentations may also have this function. This function is in addition to their role in presenting essential kinds of stimulation, as in the fields of music and language learning. Thus, one of the important uses of media is to make possible alternate modes of communication in the delivery of instruction.

We cannot here describe in any detail the kinds of audio-visual media available for instruction and their characteristic uses, strengths, and limitations. A number of texts and technical books are available on these topics, and some of them are listed at the end of this chapter. At this point, we include only a few comments on media, designed to show how they may enter into the instructional process. Decisions about the use of media must be based on what capability is being learned and how the events of instruction can best be presented when particular media are employed (Briggs, 1970; Gagné & Briggs, 1974). The following sections illustrate these ideas with *pictures*, *television programs*, and *audio cassettes*.

Pictures

Pictures are commonly used as supplements to printed texts. They may play a part in the motivation phase of instruction, although not necessarily a unique one. They may be used to direct attention to portions of a text that are to be selectively perceived. Their primary usefulness, however, occurs in the acquisition phase of instruction. Pictures are often excellent means of *coding* what is to be learned. Three kinds of coding uses for pictures are illustrated in Figure 6.1.

An obvious use of a picture is to provide an illustration of an object. The picture of the ibex serves as a coding device for many purposes for which the word "ibex" may be used in comprehending a text. The picture may be stored in the form of an image, standing in place of the defined concept "a wild goat with large curved horns." A second kind of picture is a diagram, which may be used to code an abstract concept like "focus." The student of science may readily acquire and retain "focus" by using the diagram as a code. In this case, the diagram aids in the storage and retrieval of the component concepts necessary to define the word (*i.e.* the defined concept). Without the

Figure 6.1
Three uses of pictures as coding devices in the
acquisition phase of learning.

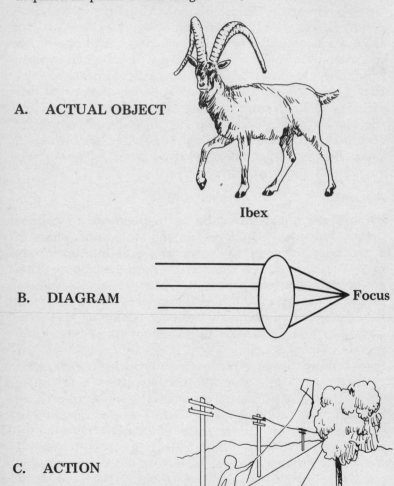

A.   **ACTUAL OBJECT**

Ibex

B.   **DIAGRAM**

Focus

C.   **ACTION**

picture, the definition would need to be retained as a verbal statement such as "a point at which rays of light meet when refracted by a lens."

Still a third use of pictures as media for the acquisition stage is shown in Figure 6.1C. Here the picture represents action, or an unfolding set of events. Quite evidently a picture of this sort aids in the comprehension and storage of a text like the following: "Donald had to run to keep the string from touching the branches of the tree. When gusts of wind came along, there was a chance for the kite to dive onto the wires, or to get entangled with a pole." Research studies have shown the particular effectiveness of pictures in performing a coding function of this sort (Bransford & Johnson, 1972; Paivio, 1971).

Television Programs

The motion pictures which may be shown via television programs have a number of potential advantages as media for instruction. Viewing television appears to be an activity which is inherently motivating. For children or adults, the desire to see events unfolding before their eyes is strong. It is a well-known fact that nearly everyone has difficulty not looking at television; and also that so long as new scenes or programs are made to appear, few people get tired of watching. The motivational features of television programs, therefore, are widely acknowledged. Some additional characteristics of television need to be considered, pertaining to its use in instruction.

Apprehending phase. The motion and abrupt changes which may be introduced in television programs are of particular use in gaining and controlling attention. This feature is used to good advantage in the series of television programs called *Sesame Street*. Each program consists of a series of brief scenes, varied in content, and many abrupt changes occur between scenes as well as within them. These techniques are highly effective in capturing and holding the attention of young children. Programs for older students and adults use similar techniques for controlling attention, although the brevity of scenes and the frequency of abrupt changes do not need to be as extreme.

Acquisition phase. Television programs are able to perform the coding functions illustrated in Figure 5.1 with great effectiveness. They can show pictures of actual objects of infinite variety and thus convey new concepts in concrete form. They can display many kinds of diagrams, including those which have moving parts. And of course they have great versatility in depicting action sequences of real or dramatized events, thus providing vivid systems for the coding of concepts and rules that are to be learned.

The learning of organized information can also be greatly aided by television presentation. The main function of the moving pictures is that of providing a meaningful context to which the learner can relate new information. Pictorial presentations can display a broad sweep of events in a relatively short space of time and thus save the student time in gaining a context for newly acquired information.

One of the most striking ways in which television programs can contribute to instruction is in the establishment and modification of attitudes. In this case, the coding function is associated with the effects of using human models. Heroes and heroines of fiction, personages of history, and political or sports figures—all can be presented in realistic form by television programs. Whatever model is chosen, it is possible for him to be seen making the choice of personal action that is to be "modeled" by the learner. Thus, the television program enormously extends the range of possible human models that can be employed to appeal to a variety of students.

Performance and feedback phases. The chief limitations of the television medium lie in its inability to require performance of the learner and to respond to this performance with feedback. Watching television may, after all, be a passive kind of activity. One cannot be certain that the learner has learned to *use* the new concept he saw on the screen. In addition, the television picture cannot make individual corrections or confirmations of the learner's performance. *Sesame Street* makes an attempt to overcome these limitations, in effect, by encouraging the young viewer to "talk back" to the screen. Thus, when the child is learning a sequence of digits ("one, two, three," etc.), he is encouraged to say them aloud and to anticipate the program voice by completing the series before "being told." Other techniques of a similar sort are used to get the child to perform and then to provide feedback for his performance. These techniques are ingenious, and they work at least part of the time.

For older students, the performance and feedback phases of instruction cannot be so easily taken care of by "talking back" procedures. Printed materials containing blanks to be filled in by the student, in response to questions or problems displayed on the television screen, are sometimes used with good effect.

Audio Tape Cassettes

The tape cassette which delivers audio messages is a highly convenient and relatively inexpensive medium. Audio cassettes are of particular usefulness in providing individualized instruction. Tape players can readily be operated by the individual student and even by young children. Not only is a considerable variety of prerecorded tapes available, but also new messages may easily be recorded to fill different instructional purposes.

It is not clear that auditory messages have a particularly valuable function in controlling attention, although this possibility should not be overlooked. When auditory instructions are interspersed with printed text, they may be useful in directing attention and in promoting selective attention by emphasizing parts of the message.

Audio tapes can be particularly useful in various phases of instructional process to communicate to learners who are too young to read, or who are not good readers. For example, children who are learning to read can in effect be "read to" by an audio tape. While hearing the story on tape, they can read along in the text and thereby confirm or correct their own attempts at identifying words. For older students who are slow readers, audio tapes are sometimes used to good advantage in communicating lesson objectives, stimulating recall, and informing students about activities to be done. Naturally, auditory messages and sounds are also of particular usefulness when the learning to be done requires this mode of communication—as, for example, with instruction in music or foreign languages.

Some Summarizing Comments

Teachers have many decisions to make in arranging for the *delivery* of instruction, over and above those that may be made when it is originally designed. Typically, instruction is delivered in three different modes—as group instruction, by tutoring, or by student self-instruction. These modes are not entirely distinct from each other, however. They are simply convenient ways of thinking about the various forms that instruction may take. Typically, the teacher who is responsible for a class of twenty-five to thirty students uses all these modes, and mixtures of them, at various times and for various purposes.

A second set of choices to be made in the delivery of instruction concerns the audio and visual media to be used. Simple forms of media like the chalkboard and the printed text are well known. Other media use materials and hardware that is more or less complex, ranging from the still picture to the computer. Media choices are best based upon the particular contributions which can be made to instruction by various audio and visual devices.

Both kinds of decisions—those for instructional mode and for audiovisual media—require careful consideration of two questions:

(1) What kind of capability is to be learned?

(2) How can the various events for instruction best be made to occur?

Absolute rules for choosing modes of instruction and

media in light of these questions are difficult to formulate. Often, the choices that are made represent genuine compromises with ideal conditions. What will be of greatest help is knowing that effective learning conditions are *different* for intellectual skills, information, cognitive strategies, attitudes, and motor skills. Each kind of learning outcome must be considered as a separate type of problem to be solved. Each requires somewhat different arrangements of the events of instruction, even though these events follow a common pattern beginning with a motivation phase and ending with feedback. In consequence, the choices of instructional modes and media are likewise found to be different for each purpose. Some learning is almost bound to occur, regardless of the teacher's decisions. The skilled teacher will be concerned to ask, "Why not make the instruction as good as possible?"

General References

Teaching Modes

Gagné R. M. *The conditions of learning.* (2nd ed.) New York: Holt, Rinehart & Winston, 1970, chapter 12.

Macmillan, C. J. B., & Nelson, T. W. (Eds.) *Concepts of teaching: Philosophical Essays.* Chicago: Rand McNally, 1968.

Postlethwait, S. N., Novak, J., & Murray, H. *An integrated experience approach to learning, with emphasis on independent study.* Minneapolis: Burgess, 1964.

Strasser, B. A conceptual model of instruction. *Journal of Teacher Education*, 1967, 18, 63-74.

Audio-Visual Media

Dale, E. *Audio-visual methods in teaching.* (3rd ed.) New York: Holt, Rinehart & Winston, 1969.

Erickson, C. W., & Curl, D. H. *Fundamentals of teaching with audio-visual technology.* (2nd ed.) New York: Macmillan, 1972.

Levie, W. H., & Dickie, K. E. The analysis and application of media. In R. M. W. Travers (Ed.), *Second handbook of research on teaching*. Chicago: Rand McNally, 1973.

Meierhenry, W. C. *Media competencies for teachers*. Lincoln, Neb.: Teachers College, University of Nebraska, 1966.

Weisgerber, R. A. (Ed.) *Instructional process and media innovation*. Chicago: Rand McNally, 1968.

Chapter 7 Self-Assessment

The reader who has arrived at this point will probably be very much aware of the need for instructional events designed to support the *performance* and *feedback* phases of learning. How are these to be carried out with respect to his own learning—the learning intended by this book?

We assume that the reader is capable of and willing to undertake self-instruction, so far as the initial phases of learning are concerned. Thus, he will have approached the reading of the previous chapters with an interest in acquiring an intellectual "model" that will enable him to organize his thinking and action relative to the instruction of others. By using his available cognitive strategies, he will have activated his attention to the sentences and paragraphs of each chapter, and will have supplied a variety of meaningful contexts useful for the coding, storage, and retrieval of intellectual skills and information.

Having done these things, the skillful student will then be inclined to ask himself, "What have I learned, and what am I going to be able to recall and use?" The questions and answers in this chapter are designed to assist the student in this task. Of course, these are not the only aids that may be available. The course instructor may have additional questions to suggest, and these in turn may lead to more extensive discussion with other students. As we have noted previously in this book, these occasions for review and variety of application will probably contribute a great deal to the retention and transfer of newly acquired knowledge and skills.

The contents of this chapter, then, may be considered as setting the stage for a process of *self-assessment* which will be continued by several other means and on a variety of occasions. The questions given here are a way of getting started. They may be undertaken chapter by chapter, if desired, or by way of a review for the entire book. Remember, though, that they are a minimal set of questions, in the sense that they cover only major points. They are designed to inform the student whether he has mastered the essentials, and at the same time to encourage him to supply the larger meaningful contexts which will aid retention and transfer. This he must do in part, at least, by drawing upon his own individual experience.

Chapter 1 - Introduction

Questions

The following set of questions will make it possible for you to check yourself on the purposes of this chapter: (a) stating why an understanding of learning is important to the teacher; (b) describing how principles of learning are obtained, verified, and incorporated into theories; (c) demonstrating by example the process of learning contained in the "basic model"; and (d) classifying examples of instruction that illustrate the usefulness of learning theory. First, go through the questions one by one and give your answers. Following this, you will find the questions repeated with answers and accompanying comments. The latter will enable you to decide whether you have mastered the point, or at least are on the right track.

---

1. Teachers promote the learning of students by *planning* and *delivering* instruction. Example: Because pupils in the first grade are observed to have difficulty reading aloud words beginning with "th" and "ph," the teacher devotes two periods of practice of words beginning with these letter combinations. Is this planning, or delivery?

. . . .

---

2. The teacher performs three primary functions in promoting learning: designing instruction, managing instruction, and assessing its effects. Which two of these might a teacher be doing in hearing a first-grader read aloud from a basal reader?

. . . .

Check Your Answers - Chapter 1

1. *Delivery.* The conduct of instruction is carried out in the two practice periods. The *planning* has been previously done; evidently the teacher has chosen this particular form of instructional delivery by planning. One would hope that the planning has been systematic, and that more than one delivery alternative has been considered.

2. *Managing* instruction, and *assessing* its effects. The first function is performed when the teacher asks for this particular performance from the child, using the particular basal reader. Obviously, assessment of the performance may also be done by listening to the performance. But the teacher has not designed this instruction—that has been done by the person who formulated the text for the basal readers.

3. Learning is an internal change of state that shows itself in changed performance, and in persistence of that change. On Wednesday, a pupil is having difficulty making the middle horizontal crossbar of an A. The teacher directs his attention to a model "A;;, and he achieves a good crossbar. Then, on Friday, he is asked to print an A. What feature of the printed A will indicate that persistence of a change (and therefore, learning) has occurred?

. . . .

4. A learning investigator intends to find out whether attention to textual passages is affected by underlining key words. He designs an experiment with suitable controls, contrasting the attention of students (as inferred from amount learned) to a paragraph on bee-raising, employing the same paragraph with and without underlining in two equivalent groups of students. In addition, he uses a second paragraph in the same way, this one dealing with the growing of corn. What quality of his observations, validity or reliability, is he seeking by including the second paragraph?

. . . .

5. Practice sometimes "makes perfect", as is the case with learning to thread a needle. In terms of *older* learning theory, what effect does repetition have on the neural connections involved?

. . . .

3. *A good horizontal crossbar.* If the child's performance in making a crossbar is initially changed for the better, this may indicate learning, or it may not. But if making a good crossbar is a change that persists over time, it is more clearly legitimate to infer that learning has taken place.

4. *Reliability.* The evidence of effects of underlining is convincing if *replication* is built into the experiment. Notice that this is done with a second paragraph, containing a different subject matter. The experimenter wants to be able to conclude that his results would be obtained with *any* subject matter; that is, that they are *reliable.* If he were concerned only with validity, this would be a matter of determining whether the differences in performance of the two groups (underline vs. no underline) were "real" ones, not attributable to chance.

5. *Strengthening.* In the older theory, connections were supposed to be strengthened by repetition. Modern theory proposes that single connections are either made or not made. Repetition may bring about a progressive *selection* of connections, and thus contribute to learning. But the single connections are not necessarily "strengthened," even though the resulting performance shows a gradual improvement.

6. According to modern learning theory, stimulation from the learner's environment affects his sense organs, and is transformed to patterns of neural "information" which are held for very brief periods in this form. What is the structure called that performs this function?

....

7. A learner has acquired and stored the skill of expressing ounces as pounds and fractions of pounds. Some days later, he is required to use this skill in comparing the contents of cans of coffee. In recalling the skill, what process is involved?

....

8. In the example of 7, if what has been learned is stored in Long-term Memory, to what structure does it flow when recall occurs?

....

9. A teacher in an inner-city school notices three things about the behavior of one pupil: A. He is usually sleepy when he arrives in the morning. B. He often does not speak distinctly enough to be understood. C. He seems to dislike doing arithmetic problems. The teacher would like to bring about changes in all three of these behaviors. To which of them (A, B, C) is knowledge of learning theory likely to be useful?

....

6. *Sensory Register.* The initial transformation of sense organ stimulation leads to very brief (of the order of hundredths of a second) neural effects, a kind of "registration" or pure "perception" of this stimulation. To be further processed, the information must be transformed and enter Short-term Memory in a "coded" form.

7. *Retrieval.* The skill of expressing ounces as pounds and fractions of pounds must be *retrieved* from Long-term Memory.

8. *Short-term Memory.* The process of retrieval frequently results in the stored skill being returned to the Short-term Memory, which is sometimes called the "working memory."

9. *B and C.* It is not obvious that learning theory can be applied to the problem of making the pupil less sleepy; the most probable, remedy is more sleep at night. It is quite probable, however, that the child can learn to speak more distinctly, and that learning theory can be employed to plan instruction for that purpose. Why does he dislike arithmetic? Perhaps it is because he has failed to learn some essential skills. Again, learning theory can aid in the identification of *what* he needs to learn, as well as in *how* he may go about the learning.

Chapter 2 - The Process of Learning

Questions

By answering the following questions, you will be able to confirm your learning of the main points of this chapter. Briefly stated, the objectives to be achieved are being able to demonstrate, by example: (a) distinctions among eight *phases* of the processing that occurs during learning, retention, and transfer of learning, and (b) relations of internal processes to the external events that may influence these processes.

As before, the questions are given in a first section. This is followed by a section in which you can check your answers and read additional comments.

1. A student has learned from his text book how to identify by name the major skeletal features of a crayfish. This *acquisition phase* of learning must have been preceded by two other phases—a motivation phase (establishing an expectancy), and what other phase?

....

2. In the example of 1, assuming what has been learned has entered the Long-term Memory, what is the essential learning process called?

....

3. In the example of 1, the process of learning may have involved the formulation of meaningful sentences by the learner such as "leg joints ending in a claw like a thumb and opposing finger." What is another possibility for the form of this essential process of the acquisition phase?

....

Check Your Answers - Chapter 2

1. *Apprehending Phase*. That is, the phase in which external stimulation is attended to and perceived. If you answered "attention" or "perception," these are not so bad. However, they are names for the processes involved in the apprehending phase.

2. *Coding*. What is sought as an answer here is the name for the process. Entry into long-term memory is accomplished by the process of coding.

3. *Image, or imagery*. Coding can be done in verbal terms, and often is. However, generating an image, usually a visual image, can be a very effective coding process. In this particular instance, in which the parts of a structure are being learned, an image may work particularly well.

4. A student has learned the old names of seven East African countries, and now is faced with the necessity of learning the "new" names of the same countries, since they have recently been changed. He learns the new names, but often confuses them with the old ones when he needs to recall them. What is this phenomenon called?

. . . .

5. A teacher wants students to recall the functions of a city council, and mentions the words "legislative, executive, judicial." In doing this, the teacher is providing an external cue for what process?

. . . .

6. Having learned about several kinds of "figures of speech" in English writing, students are given a number of different verses of poetry, and asked to identify the figures of speech within them. What learning process is being supported by this kind of instructional event?

. . . .

7. Students have been given the assignment of describing the physical properties of a metal which could best be used for the body of a moon landing vehicle, based upon what they have previously learned about the moon's environment and about metals. Their descriptions are returned by the teacher with comments about the number of metallic properties listed. Is this feedback adequate or inadequate?

. . . .

4. *Interference*. This is an important fact about retention, well-known in everyone's experience. Presumably, this confusion of "old" and "new" learning occurs within the storage phase, as a characteristic of long-term memory. However, it needs to be carefully distinguished from "failure of retrieval," which may occur for quite different reasons; for example, the absence or loss of good "retrieval cues."

5. *Retrieval*. The cues provided by the teacher serve the function of activating the process of retrieval of the three branches of government. Acting on these cues, students will be able to recall what they have learned about the function of each branch of city government.

6. *Transfer,* or *transfer of learning*. The students have learned to identify examples of particular kinds of figures of speech. Now, in this generalization phase, they are given verses of poetry which they have not previously encountered, and are asked to apply their newly learned skills.

7. *Inadequate*. Such feedback does not clearly relate to the objective of solving a novel problem. The statement of the problem implied that the students should think out and justify the appropriateness of certain metallic properties. Thus, quality of thought was the expectancy established. To provide feedback only on the number of properties listed is to turn a valuable exercise in problem solving into routine list-retrieval.

8. When an inexperienced person first looks through a microscope, he is likely to "see" little except an undifferentiated field of view. Assuming he expects to learn to identify parts of the structure he is looking at, what is the first process of learning that must be carried out?

. . . .

9. A student has been learning to identify trees in his local area. On a field trip, he correctly identifies nine out of ten different trees that are pointed at by the teacher. The feedback identifies for the student which trees were spotted correctly and which were not (as opposed to the statement "That's very good.") What kind of feedback is this?

. . . .

10. In learning how to compute compound interest, students are first given a few examples of converting fractional numbers to percents. In this case, retrieval is brought about to aid the learning of a new skill. To what structure is the previously learned skill retrieved?

. . . .

8. *Discrimination,* or *perceptual learning.* Before identification of parts of the structure can be learned, the student must learn to distinguish shapes, edges, and textures in the field he is viewing. Having done this, he is ready to learn to identify such "things" as cells, cell nuclei, and others.

9. *Informational feedback.* Telling the student he is "doing very well" is not effective reinforcement, even though it has the appearance of being rewarding. What works best is specific information about which trees he has been able to identify, and what he missed.

10. *Short-term memory, or working memory.* Presumably, students have stored the skill of expressing fractional numbers as decimals in long-term memory. Now it must be incorporated into the learning of a new and more complex skill. To be made more readily accessible, the previously learned skill is retrieved from long-term memory back into short-term memory.

Chapter 3 - The Outcomes of Learning

Questions

By answering the following questions, you will be able to check your learning of the main ideas of Chapter 3. You should be able to name and give examples of the five major categories of learning outcomes, as well as certain subordinate categories like *concept* and *rule*.

1. This chapter deals with the effects of learning as the establishment of a *persisting internal state*. What is the general name for this kind of internal state?

....

2. A pupil in the fourth grade learns the capability of using the apostrophe to signify "possession," as in "the tree's branches." If he can use the apostrophe correctly, what major category of capability does this represent?

....

3. A teacher finds that, as a result of instruction, students have come to prefer five minutes of silent reading in class to a similar amount of oral reading by individuals. What general category of learning outcome is this?

....

Check Your Answers - Chapter 3

---

1. *Capabilities.* The internal change produced by learning is a change of state (of the human nervous system) which *persists.* Since this state makes certain behavior possible, we call it a *capability.*

---

2. *An intellectual skill.* The capability makes it possible for the learner to respond to a class of situations with a consistency that makes us call his behavior "rule-governed." In other words, he is able to use the apostrophe to signify "possession" regardless of what is possessed or of who or what is the possessor. It is a skill involving the use of language, which we call an intellectual skill. The specific type of skill is called a rule; but the question asks for the major category.

---

3. *Attitude.* The students are making a choice, or expressing a preference, for a kind of action which includes their own. The question doesn't tell you how instruction managed to establish this preference, but that is a later story. But as a learned outcome, it is clearly an attitude.

---

4. Two students, A and B, have both mastered finding the area of a rectangle equally well. Now a novel situation is presented: they are shown a diagram and are asked to find the area of a parallelogram. B does this correctly more readily and more quickly than A. In what major category of capability might A and B differ?

. . . .

5. Having studied the first amendment to the U.S. Constitution, students are able to answer the question, "What is prohibited by the first amendment?" Identify the type of learned capability.

. . . .

6. When the teacher asks pupils to "mark the ones that are triangles" in a group of geometric figures, what is being observed is an intellectual skill called what?

. . . .

7. Students in geometry classes sometimes learn to draw a large circle on the chalkboard with a continuous stroke. What is this kind of capability?

. . . .

4. *Cognitive strategy (or strategies).* If they really have mastered the skill of finding the area of a rectangle equally well, it is reasonable to suppose that B has some *strategies* of learning and thinking which are not available to A. B is able to attack the problem in some better, more efficient way, and so does it more readily and more quickly. Were you perhaps tempted to say, B has more "intelligence"? It would be easier to reply to such an answer if we knew better what "intelligence" is. As a guess, couldn't we argue that the effectiveness of a person's cognitive strategies for learning and thinking comes pretty close to what we mean by intelligence?

5. *Verbal information.* The teacher is asking the students to *state* something, that something being the main ideas of the first amendment. Notice that the teacher doesn't ask the students to "recite", or to repeat verbatim. The ideas (propositions) are what are being sought as a learned capability.

6. *Concrete concept.* The concept "triangle" is being identified by the pupils, and this is a subordinate category of intellectual skill. If you were tempted to say discrimination, this would not be correct. Notice that the pupils must not only distinguish (or discriminate) triangles from other figures which are different, but they must also *classify* the correct ones as "triangles." In other words, they must have learned "triangle" as a concrete concept. Later on, perhaps, in a geometry class, they will also learn "triangle" as a defined concept.

7. *Motor skill.* Have you ever learned to draw such a circle on a chalkboard with a single stroke? It is a motor skill, and it takes practice to establish it.

8. A lesson on "drug abuse" deals with the common names of harmful drugs, and their effects on the human body. What kind of capability is being learned?

. . . .

9. A student has learned to add −3 and +5; he has also learned to add all other sets of positive and negative numbers. What kind of intellectual skill is this?

. . . .

10. A student has learned to remember people's names by making them rhyme with a familiar word. Would you call this an intellectual skill or a cognitive strategy?

. . . .

8. *Verbal information*. The names and effects of drugs constitute a set of information which the students can later state (or tell about). It is possible that the intention here is to establish an attitude. But the contents of the lesson as described are verbal information. More than this will be needed to change attitudes.

9. *Rule*. The student has learned the capability of "adding directed numbers (integers)." He responds to an entire class of numbers by applying rules. Notice that this doesn't necessarily mean he can *state* the rules—that would be the capability called verbal information. But he can use the rules, or demonstrate their use.

10. *Cognitive strategy*. This may be a relatively simple cognitive strategy, and one of limited usefulness. Nevertheless, it is an internally organized skill which governs the learner's own remembering processes. It is not an intellectual skill, because it is not a matter of applying a specific rule or concept to the names remembered. Instead, one could say that the student is making up a new concept whenever he makes up a rhyme for a new name. Thus, he is using a cognitive strategy to enhance his own recall of names.

Chapter 4 - Conditions for Learning

Questions

Check your learning of the ideas of Chapter 4 by answering the following questions and comparing your answers with those given. From a study of this chapter, you should be able to identify good statements of objectives for each type of learning outcome. Then, in addition, your knowledge of this chapter should enable you to identify the critical conditions for the promotion of each kind of learning outcome.

---

1. In the learning objective "Given the printed sentence 'The rain had been heavy yet the grass protected as it was by the cliff was scarcely wet', demonstrates punctuation with commas by writing them in appropriate places", the outcome performance is described by what word?

....

---

2. In the example of a learning objective given in question 1, what kind of learning outcome is being described?

....

---

3. In the incomplete learning objective, "Given the question, 'What became of the territory of Austria-Hungary after World War I?', _____ the new countries formed", what is the appropriate major verb, and to what kind of learning outcome does it refer?

....

Check Your Answers - Chapter 4

---

1. *Demonstrates*. This is the major verb in the sentence, which describes the kind of learning outcome to be expected. In other words, this verb tells what kind of capability is being learned. Notice that there is also a minor verb—"by writing" —which simply tells what specific action is to be performed.

---

2. *A rule*. The verb demonstrate implies that this variety of intellectual skill is being learned. This learner will be able to exhibit performances (using commas to punctuate sentences) which are "rule-governed."

---

3. *States*. Clearly, the learning outcome intended is verbal information. We expect students who have learned such information to be able to state it, orally or in writing.

---

4. In the learning of the intellectual skill of finding the length of a hypotenuse, some subordinate skills are (a) finding the square of a number and (b) finding the square root of a number. Assuming these simpler skills have been previously learned, what must happen to them just before the new skill is learned?

. . . .

5. A teacher has told her students that successful problem solving is aided by learning how to "clarify the essentials of the problem." What else should be done in order to bring about the desired learning outcome?

. . . .

6. In learning to put a parked automobile in motion, the novice driver must learn to signal and to look both ways before accelerating to move the car into the street lane. What component of a motor skill do these actions represent?

. . . .

7. Facts about agricultural products of the State of Missouri are introduced in the context of topographic and climatic conditions of that state. According to theory, what learning process is supported by this context?

. . . .

4. *Retrieval*. According to learning theory, these subordinate skills must be retrieved to the working memory. When made accessible in this way, the subordinate skills are ready to be combined in new learning of the more complex skill.

5. *Practice with varied examples*. Actually, simply telling the students that they need to clarify the essentials of a problem has little effectiveness in and of itself. They need to be provided with frequent opportunities to carry out such clarifications, in problem situations that challenge them to do so.

6. *An executive subroutine*. Of course, the performance of putting the car into the street lane has to be done with the smoothness and timing characteristic of a motor skill. But in addition, such a skill incorporates the procedures of signalling, looking, etc., which are referred to as an executive subroutine. The motor performance is exhibited within the framework of this routine.

7. *Coding*. The larger meaningful context is presented along with the specific facts about agricultural products. The effect of this context, which might be accompanied by a topographic map, is to make possible an effective coding of the information. Later on, when the facts are retrieved, this context will provide valuable cues to memory.

8. For a group of high-school students, who would be more likely as a human model to influence attitudes—the governor of the state or the captain of the football team?

. . . .

9. When an intellectual skill such as "changing inches to centimeters" is being learned, new examples are often presented in spaced reviews. What learning process is this procedure designed to support?

. . . .

10. A teacher asks students to bring to bear their most original thoughts in preparing a short paper on "morality in politics." The papers are then graded primarily in terms of spelling and punctuation. What principle of effective learning conditions is being violated here?

. . . .

8. *The football captain.* Such a person is likely to be better known than the governor, and to be more universally admired. Therefore, he may be a more likely model with whom students would "identify." Of course, there are circumstances in which this situation could be reversed. Also remember that parents, teachers, and even fictional characters can become human models for changes in attitudes. The early high school years, though, are likely to be characterized by a certain amount of rejection of adult models.

9. *Retrieval.* Practice in applying the skill to additional examples, spaced over time, has been shown to have marked positive effects on retrieval. The spacing appears to be an important feature of this practice, probably because the most useful cues to retrieval are in a sense "practiced" by this means.

10. *Specificity of feedback.* If the students have been asked to "be original", the feedback should tell them how original they have been. Otherwise, their use of desirable cognitive strategies will not be reinforced. There is nothing wrong, of course, with indicating errors in punctuation and spelling. But when this becomes the primary kind of feedback (as in this example), the instructional purpose of the exercise is defeated.

Chapter 5 - Planning Instruction

Questions

The following self-test questions will provide you with the opportunity of confirming or correcting your learning of the main points of Chapter 5. You should be able to describe how the planning of courses and topics can take learning principles into account. Then, in considering the design of lessons, we expect you will have learned how to identify and arrange the events of instruction for the most effective support of learning.

---

1. In a social studies course, a possible topic is Family Differences. Besides the goal of providing information about families in various cultures, what other goal is such a topic likely to have?

. . . .

---

2. In an experimental program, School A has decided to try teaching the basic principles of trigonometry to fifth grade students. What aspect of support for learning is likely to be prominent in course planning?

. . . .

---

3. In taking account of prerequisites for a topic on volcanoes, planning is made for a prior lesson dealing with such concepts as "cone", "magma", "lava", etc. What kind of prerequisite learning does this prior lesson represent?

. . . .

Check Your Answers - Chapter 5

---

1. *Attitude learning.* Usually information about differences in families of various cultures is not taught solely for its own sake. It is often a prerequisite to the learning of an attitude of tolerance toward family differences. Of course, unless the youngster first learns that there *are* many kinds of differences in families, he can hardly be expected to learn to be tolerant of them.

---

2. *Sequence of prerequisites.* Although it is not clear why anyone would propose to teach trigonometry in the fifth grade, there is no good reason why it couldn't be done. What would mainly be required is being sure that the pupils had previously learned a number of rules of arithmetic and geometry, presented in a suitable sequence, before they attempted to learn trigonometric rules.

---

3. *Concept learning, or the referent meanings of words.* If new information is to be learned, it is frequently a prerequisite that the component words be learned as concepts. When this is done, sentences about volcanoes will be immediately "understood"; otherwise, they are unlikely to be.

---

4. In learning the motor skills involved in the game of tennis, specific practice is often given to the "backhand stroke." What kind of a prerequisite is this?

....

5. In introducing a speaker for a special program on traffic safety, the principal places considerable emphasis on the speaker's previous experience as a racing driver. What kind of a prerequisite is of major concern here?

....

6. A textbook chapter on Trees of North America contains diagrams with arrows pointing to labeled features such as *bark, branching, roots,* and *leaves.* What learning function do these arrows serve?

....

7. The plan for teaching the territorial extents of major tribes of American Indians calls for the use of a labeled map as a suggested coding scheme. What kind of "event of instruction" does the introduction of this map represent?

....

8. Once the rule of "doubling the consonant before 'ing' " has been learned, the teacher waits a couple of days before asking the students to apply the rule to several new examples. What is this procedure called?

....

4. *Part-skills learning* is often a prerequisite to the acquisition of a complex motor skill. You can probably think of many examples, besides tennis, which illustrate this point.

5. *Identification with a human model.* At least, this is what the principal is trying to achieve, with the greatest possible number of students, when he introduces the speaker as a former racing driver. Would he achieve the same effect with a speaker who was a former policeman?

6. *Directing attention.* Obviously, it is often rather easy to bring about this instructional event, whether by diagrams, printed sentences, or oral directions.

7. *Providing learning guidance.* The provision of a coding scheme, or the suggestion of one, is frequently the way in which learning guidance is used to support internal learning processes.

8. *Spaced review.* The teacher is asking the students to recall the rule by applying it to new examples. By this means, the internal processes of search and retrieval are brought fully into play. The "spaced" aspect of the review is important and presumably for this reason.

9, When the student of a foreign language constructs sentences using the definite article, the teacher points out the correct instances and corrects the errors, rather than saying "that was fairly good." What kind of feedback is the former?

....

10. What kind of capability makes it possible for the self-instructed learner to provide himself with such events as stimulating recall and guidance for learning?

....

9. *Informativefeedback*. This is the kind of feedback which most adequately confirms the expectancy the learner has acquired at the beginning of learning. Reinforcement is thus provided to complete the learning act.

10. *Cognitive strategies*. These "executive processes" are brought to bear by the learner on other processes of learning. They provide internal cues which guide learning and retrieval. The effective use of cognitive strategies shows that the student has "learned to learn", in a self-instructional way.

Chapter 6 - Delivering Instruction

Questions

Here is a set of self-test questions for Chapter 6. Having studied this chapter, you should be able to describe what various things the teacher does to support the internal processes of learning. Further, it should be possible for you to exemplify how they are done with a class, in tutorial instruction, and with individual learning. Finally, we hope you have learned something about the characteristics of audio and visual presentations as parts of instruction.

---

1. Three modes of instructional delivery are class instruction, tutoring, and individual study. Which two of these are used for instruction in piano playing?

....

---

2. Out of a total adult class in Spanish language, three different smaller groups are formed: (a) those who speak Spanish at home; (b) those who can read Spanish but cannot speak it; (c) those who can neither read nor speak Spanish. What kind of individual differences are represented by these groupings?

....

---

3. Hinting and prompting, without providing the answer, is often done differently with different students in a class; what phase of instruction is this?

....

Check Your Answers - Chapter 6

1. *Tutoring and individual study*. Class instruction in piano would be difficult indeed to do with any degree of effectiveness, because of the individual differences in the students— how much they already know how to do, how rapidly they acquire part-skills, etc. Of course, for similar reasons, tutoring and individual study are appropriate for instruction in other subjects, also.

2. *Differences in entering capabilities*. The teacher in this case has recognized the difficulties of arranging good instruction for students with such prominent differences that they "bring with them" to the class. The small groups make it possible for the members of each to begin their learning at approximately the same point.

3. *Providing learning guidance*. The hints and prompts support the process of learning (that is, coding). Because of differences in their previous learning, such guidance often needs to be different for different students.

4. In a class discussion on the fairness of the U.S. income tax, one or two students ask for clarification of the statement (made by another student) that living in a mortgaged home often provides a tax advantage. What is being shown by the questioning students?

....

5. Having assigned a lesson on sources of electric power, a teacher is concerned that eliciting answers in class from certain eager students is likely to prevent other students from receiving feedback on their own performances. What can the teacher do to provide feedback for all?

....

6. In carrying out the action of "stimulating recall", a teacher may remind the class of some previously learned information useful for their next learning task. In contrast, how is recall likely to be stimulated in an individual tutoring situation?

....

7. A student engaged in individual learning about electrical resistance and its effect on the flow of current reminds himself of the analogy of resistance to size of pipe (for the flow of water). This enhances his retention of the relationship he has learned. What instructional function is the student performing for himself?

....

4. *Absence of relevant prerequisite knowledge.* If a discussion of the fairness of the income tax is to be successful, all students should come to the class with knowledge of how income tax is calculated, including its provisions for exemptions, deductions, etc. The students who must ask to be informed about these provisions are interfering with effective discussion.

5. *Give a quiz.* By this means, the teacher will provide each student an opportunity to perform on his own, without waiting for the answers of other students, and to receive feedback which is appropriate to his performance.

6. *Asking the student to recall the relevant information.* The tutor is likely, first, to identify rather precisely what prerequisite information is needed by the student, and second, to set the student the task of recalling it. The teacher's reminder is obviously a less precise way of stimulating recall, which will perhaps work with most students, but not with all.

7. *Supplying his own retrieval cues.* The visual image of the pipe and its effect on the flow of water may serve as an effective cue to retrieve the more abstract concept of electrical resistance.

---

8. A tutor in elementary algebra has provided a variety of hints and prompts to aid his student in learning how to multiply expressions like $a^3 \times a^5 = ?$ But the student does not learn this skill readily. What should the tutor do?

. . . .

---

9. A diagram is used to illustrate the flow of cold air in an air-conditioned room. What internal process of learning is supported by the use of such a diagram?

. . . .

---

10. In a televised lesson on navigation with a compass, a lecturer demonstrates the correct procedures in several instances. A workbook is also provided for the viewing students, in which they respond to questions posed by the lecturer, later having a chance to hear the correct answers. What learning function does the workbook serve?

. . . .

---

8. *Look for missing subordinate skills.* In the situation described, the idea that one or more subordinate intellectual skills may not be accessible is the most likely possibility. For example, is the student able to express a^3 as $a \cdot a \cdot a$? Is he able to write the whole expression as $(a \cdot a \cdot a)(a \cdot a \cdot a)$? These are two subordinate skills that might be looked for. Once a diagnosis is confirmed, of course, the tutor can then proceed to teach the missing skills.

9. *Coding.* The diagram suggests to the learner a way of coding the information about the flow of cold air. In this sense it may take the place of several verbal propositions.

10. *Performance and feedback.* These are particularly difficult phases of learning to bring about solely by means of a television picture. The supplementary materials presented in a workbook, though, accomplish these functions very well, thus enhancing the learning effectiveness of the television program.

References

Adams, J.A. *Human memory*. New York: McGraw-Hill, 1967.

Anderson, J.R., & Bower, G.H. Recognition and retrieval processes in free recall. *Psychological Review*, 1972, 79, 97-123.

Atkinson, R.C., & Shiffrin, R.M. Human memory: A proposed system and its control processes. In K.W. Spence & J.T. Spence (Eds.), *The psychology of learning and motivation*. Vol. II. New York: Academic Press, 1968.

Ausubel, D.P. *Educational psychology: A cognitive view*. New York: Holt, Rinehart & Winston, 1968.

Ausubel, D.P., & Fitzgerald, D. The role of discriminability in meaningful verbal learning and retention. *Journal of Educational Psychology*, 1961, 52, 266-274.

Bandura, A. *Principles of behavior modification*. New York: Holt, Rinehart & Winston, 1969.

Bandura, A. Vicarious and self-reinforcement processes. In R. Glaser (Ed.), *The nature of reinforcement.* New York: Academic Press, 1971.

Bloom, B.S., Hastings, J.T., & Madaus, G.F. *Handbook on formative and summative evaluation of human learning.* New York: McGraw-Hill, 1971.

Bower, G.H. Mental imagery and associative learning. In L. Gregg (Ed.), *Cognition in learning and memory.* New York: Wiley, 1971.

Bransford, J.D., & Johnson, M.K. Contextual prerequisites for understanding: Some investigations of comprehension and recall. *Journal of Verbal Learning and Verbal Behavior,* 1972, 11, 717-726.

Briggs, L.J. *Handbook of procedures for the design of instruction.* Pittsburgh, Pa.: American Institutes for Research, 1970.

Bruner, J.S. *Toward a theory of instruction.* Cambridge: Harvard University Press, 1966.

Bruner, J.S. *The relevance of education.* New York: Norton, 1971.

Carmichael, L., Hogan, H.F., & Walter, A.A. An experimental study of the effect of language on the reproduction of visually perceived form. *Journal of Experimental Psychology,* 1932, 15, 73-86.

Covington, M.V., Crutchfield, R.S., Davies, L.B., & Olton, R.M. *The productive thinking program.* Columbus, Ohio: Merrill, 1972.

Crovitz, H.F. *Galton's walk.* New York: Harper & Row, 1970.

Dale, E. *Audio-visual methods in teaching.* (3rd ed.) New York: Holt, Rinehart & Winston, 1969.

Deese, J., & Hulse, S.H. *The psychology of learning.* (3rd ed.) New York: McGraw-Hill, 1967.

Ellson, D.G., Barber, L., Engle, T.L., & Kanpwerth, L. Programmed tutoring: A teaching aid and a research tool. *Reading Research Quarterly,* 1965, 1, 77-127.

Ellson, D.G., Harris, P., & Barber, L. A field test of programed and directed tutoring. *Reading Research Quarterly,* 1968, 3, 307-367.

Erickson, C.W., & Curl, D.H. *Fundamentals of teaching with audio-visual technology*. (2nd ed.) New York: Macmillan, 1972.

Estes, W.K. All-or-none processes in learning and retention. *American Psychologist*, 1964, 19, 16-25.

Estes, W.K. Reinforcement in human behavior. *American Scientist*, 1972, 60, 723-729.

Fishbein, M. (Ed.) *Attitude theory and measurement*. New York: Wiley, 1967.

Fitts, P.M., & Posner, M.J. *Human performance*. Belmont, Calif.: Brooks/Cole, 1967.

Flavell, J.H. *The developmental psychology of Jean Piaget*. Princeton, N.J.: Van Nostrand, 1963.

Gagné R.M. Context, isolation and interference effects on the retention of fact. *Journal of Educational Psychology*, 1968, 60, 408-414.

Gagné R.M. *The conditions of learning*. (2nd ed.) New York: Holt, Rinehart & Winston, 1970.

Gagné R.M. Domains of learning. *Interchange*, 1972, 3, 1-8.

Gagné R.M., & Briggs, L.J. *Principles of instructional design*. New York: Holt, Rinehart & Winston, 1974.

Gagné R.M., & Fleishman, E.A. *Psychology and human performance*. New York: Holt, Rinehart & Winston, 1959.

Gartner, A., Kohler, M.G., & Riessman, F. *Children teach children. Learning by teaching*. New York: Harper & Row, 1971.

Gibson, E.J. *Principles of perceptual learning and development*. New York: Appleton-Century-Crofts, 1969.

Gibson, J.J. The reproduction of visually perceived forms. *Journal of Experimental Psychology*, 1929, 12, 1-39.

Glaser, R. Learning and the technology of instruction. *AV Communication Review*, 1961, 9, 42-55.

Haslerud, G.M. *Transfer, memory & creativity*. Minneapolis: University of Minnesota Press, 1973.

Hebb, D.O. *A textbook of psychology*. (3rd ed.) Philadelphia: Saunders, 1972.

Hendrickson, G., & Schroeder, W.H. Transfer of training

in learning to hit a submerged target. *Journal of Educational Psychology*, 1941, 32, 205-213.

Hilgard, E.R., & Bower, G.V. *Theories of Learning.* (4th ed.) New York: Appleton-Century-Crofts, 1974.

Hill, W.F. *Learning: A survey of psychological interpretations.* San Francisco: Chandler, 1963.

Homme, L., Csanyi, A., Gonzales, M., & Rechs, J. *How to use contingency contracting in the classroom.* Champaign, Ill.: Research Press, 1970.

Jensen, A.R., & Rohwer, W.D., Jr. Verbal mediation in paired-associate and serial learning. *Journal of Verbal Learning and Verbal Behavior*, 1963, 1, 346-352.

Johnson, D.M. *Systematic introduction to the psychology of thinking.* New York: Harper & Row, 1972.

Judd, C.H. The relation of special training to general intelligence. *Educational Review*, 1908, 36, 28-42.

Katona, G. *Organizing and memorizing.* New York: Columbia University Press, 1940.

Kimble, G.A. *Hilgard and Marquis' conditioning and learning.* (2nd ed.) New York: Appleton-Century-Crofts, 1961.

Krasner, L., & Ullman, L.P. *Research in behavior modification: New developments and implications.* New York: Holt, Rinehart & Winston, 1965.

Krathwohl, D.R., Bloom, B.S., & Masia, B.B. *Taxonomy of educational objectives. Handbook II: Affective domain.* New York: McKay, 1964.

Levie, W.H., & Dickie, K.E. The analysis and application of media. In R.M.W. Travers (Ed.), *Second handbook of research on teaching.* Chicago: Rand McNally, 1973.

Levin, J.R., Davidson, R.E., Wolff, P., & Citron, M. A comparison of induced imagery and sentence strategies in children's paired-associate learning. *Journal of Educational Psychology*, 1973, 64, 306-309.

Levin, J.R., & Kaplan, S.A. Imaginal facilitation of paired-associate learning: a limited generalization? *Journal of Educational Psychology*, 1972, 63, 429-432.

Lindsay, P.H., & Norman, D.A. *Human information*

processing: An introduction to psychology. New York: Academic Press, 1972.

Macmillan, C.J.B., & Nelson, T.W. (Eds.). *Concepts of teaching: Philosophical essays*. Chicago: Rand McNally, 1968.

Mager, R.F. *Preparing objectives for instruction*. Belmont, Calif.: Fearon, 1962.

Mager, R.F. *Developing attitude toward learning*. Belmont, Calif.: Fearon, 1968.

Meierhenry, W.C. *Media competencies for teachers*. Lincoln, Nebr.: Teachers College, University of Nebraska, 1966.

Merrill, M.D. *Instructional design: Readings*. Englewood Cliffs, N.J.: Prentice-Hall, 1971.

Merrill, M.D. Paradigms for psychomotor instruction. In M.D. Merrill (Ed.), *Instructional design: Readings*. Englewood Cliffs, N.J.: Prentice-Hall, 1971.

Niedermeyer, F.C., & Ellis, P.A. *Development of a tutorial program for kindergarten reading instruction*. Los Alamitos, Calif.: Southwest Regional Laboratory, 1970.

Norman, D.A. (Ed.) *Models of human memory*. New York: Academic Press, 1970.

Nuthall, G., & Snook, I. Contemporary models of teaching. In R.M.W. Travers (Ed.), *Second handbook of research on teaching*. Chicago: Rand McNally, 1973.

Olton, R.M., & Crutchfield, R.S. Developing the skills of productive thinking. In P. Mussen, J. Langer, & M. Covington (Eds.), *Trends and issues in developmental psychology*. New York: Holt, Rinehart & Winston, 1969.

Paivio, A. *Imagery and verbal processes*. New York: Holt, Rinehart & Winston, 1971.

Popham, W.J., & Baker, E.L. *Planning an instructional sequence*. Englewood Cliffs, N.J.: Prentice-Hall, 1970.

Popham, W.J., & Baker, E.L. *Systematic instruction*. Englewood Cliffs, N.J.: Prentice-Hall, 1970.

Postlethwait, S.N., Novak, J., & Murray, H. *An integrated experience approach to learning, with emphasis on independent study*. Minneapolis: Burgess, 1964.

Reynolds, J.H., & Glaser, R. Effects of repetition and spaced review upon retention of a complex learning task. *Journal of Educational Psychology*, 1964, 55, 297-308.

Rohwer, W.D., Jr. Elaboration and learning in childhood and adolescence. In H.W. Reese (Ed.), *Advances in child development and behavior*. New York: Academic Press, 1974.

Rohwer, W.D., Jr., & Lynch, S. Semantic constraint in paired-associate learning. *Journal of Educational Psychology*, 1966, 57, 271-278.

Shulman, L.S., & Keislar, E.R. *Learning by discovery: A critical appraisal*. Chicago: Rand McNally, 1966.

Singer, R.N. *Psychomotor domain: Movement behavior*. Philadelphia: Lea & Febiger, 1972.

Skinner, B.F. *The technology of teaching*. New York: Appleton-Century-Crofts, 1968.

Smith, B.O. A concept of teaching. *Teachers College Record*, 1960, 61, 229-241.

Stephens, J.M., & Evans, E.D. *Development and classroom learning: An introduction to educational psychology*. New York: Holt, Rinehart & Winston, 1973.

Strasser, B. A conceptual model of instruction. *Journal of Teacher Education*, 1967, 18, 63-74.

Thorndike, E.L. *Educational psychology. Vol. II: The psychology of learning*. New York: Teachers College, Columbia University, 1921.

Travers, R.M.W. *Essentials of learning*. (3rd ed.) New York: Macmillan, 1972.

Tulving, E., & Donaldson, W. (Eds.) *Organization of memory*. New York: Academic Press, 1972.

Tulving, E. & Pearlstone, Z. Availability versus accessibility of information in memory for words. *Journal of Verbal Learning and Verbal Behavior*, 1966, 5, 381-391.

Tyler, R.W. *Basic principles of curriculum and instruction*. Chicago: University of Chicago Press, 1949.

Weisgerber, R.A. (Ed.) *Instructional process and media innovation*. Chicago: Rand McNally, 1968.

White, R.W. Motivation reconsidered: The concept of competence. *Psychological Review*, 1959, 66, 297-333.

Woodworth, R.S. *Experimental psychology*. New York: Holt, Rinehart & Winston, 1938.

Index

Essentials of Learning for Instruction

Expanded Edition

Robert M. Gagné
Florida State University

The Dryden Press
Hinsdale, Illinois